Form and
Content of
Company
Accounts

Form and
Content of
Company
Accounts

Comprehensive coverage of disclosure requirements of
Companies Acts 1948–1981, SSAPs and the Listing
Agreement

Coopers
&Lybrand

First published in Great Britain 1982 by Financial Training Publications
Limited, Avenue House, 131 Holland Park Avenue, London W11 4UT.

© Coopers & Lybrand, 1982

ISBN: 0 906322 14 6

Contents

Contents

Acknowledgement

The publishers acknowledge with thanks Her Majesty's Stationery Office's kind permission to reproduce the balance sheet and profit and loss account formats from the Companies Act 1981.

Preface

The disclosure requirements for the accounts of British companies are derived from an ever increasing number of sources. As a result, the preparer or auditor of accounts finds it more and more difficult to perform the task of ensuring that these requirements are met.

The main purpose of this book is to bring together the statutory and other disclosure requirements for company accounts, including those introduced by the Companies Act 1981. It contains an explanatory guide to the disclosure requirements, together with specimen accounts prepared under the new rules, and a checklist. This checklist provides a ready means of determining whether or not accounts comply with the various disclosure requirements.

In addition, the book deals in Chapter 12 with the provisions of the 1980 and 1981 Acts relating to capital and distributions. Although these provisions do not relate to the disclosure requirements for accounts, they are included because they will be of interest to those concerned with accounts. A summary of the legal requirements for statutory books, the filing of accounts and certain other matters is included in Chapter 11.

1 Introduction

General

1   The Companies Act 1981 received the Royal Assent on 30 October 1981, and is now being brought into effect by Statutory Instrument. The provisions relating to disclosure requirements are expected to be introduced early in 1982, and will apply to accounting periods commencing after the relevant order has been issued.

2   The principal objective of the 1981 Act was to introduce into British law the requirements of the EEC Fourth Directive. It has resulted in substantial changes being made both to accounting disclosure requirements and to other company law issues. This book concentrates principally upon disclosure requirements.

3   The main provisions of the Companies Act 1981, as they apply to the form and content of company accounts, are:

(a) a requirement to produce accounts for the shareholders in a specified format, with fuller disclosure than in the past;

(b) an option for certain smaller companies to produce 'modified' (i.e. shortened) accounts for filing with the registrar of companies;

(c) a requirement to adopt certain accounting principles and policies, although current best practice is largely unaltered;

(d) an obligation to give in the directors' report fuller information about the activities of the company, on the lines of that often found in the chairman's statement;

(e) the recognition in statute of the concept of the 'related' or associated company; and

(f) the exemption of dormant companies from audit.

4   It is also important to note that the Companies Act 1981 has stipulated that the prime requirement must be for accounts to give a 'true and fair view'. To that end the accounts must, if necessary, provide further information not otherwise required, or even override the disclosure provisions of the Act.

5   No definition of a true and fair view is provided in statute, but it is generally accepted that, to give such a view, accounts must:

    (a)   be prepared on the basis of the four fundamental accounting concepts;

    (b)   employ appropriate accounting policies consistently applied;

    (c)   present an overall picture that is not in any way misleading;

    (d)   disclose all information material to a proper understanding of the accounts;

    (e)   describe the amounts in the accounts in such a way that their true nature is explained unambiguously; and

    (f)   strike a balance between completeness of disclosure and the summarisation necessary for clarity.

6   If the accounts are prepared on bases which differ in material respects from any of the four generally accepted fundamental accounting concepts (*viz* going concern, accruals, consistency and prudence) the facts must be explained, together with the reasons for the departure and the effects thereof. (This requirement is contained in paragraphs 10 to 15 of the first schedule to the Companies Act 1981, and in paragraphs 14 and 17 of SSAP 2.)

Sources of Disclosure Requirements

7   The Companies Acts 1948 to 1981 lay down minimum statutory requirements for the preparation of accounts of companies. These requirements are supplemented by:

    (a)   Statements of Standard Accounting Practice; and
    (b)   The Stock Exchange Listing Agreement (for listed companies only).

8   This book summarises the accounts disclosure requirements contained in the above, and also contains suggestions made by the authors as to best practice where there is difficulty in interpreting the statutory requirements or where additional disclosure may be desirable. Where no statutory or other authority for a paragraph is indicated in the reference column, the comments in that paragraph are those of the authors. In cases where a paragraph contains both a statutory or other requirement and the authors' comments, this is indicated in the reference column.

9   In addition, certain legislative requirements in connection with a company's accounts are dealt with although they do not strictly relate to disclosure (e.g. the Companies Acts' regulations on the filing of accounts).

10   This edition includes requirements published up to 31 December 1981. In cases of difficulty, reference should always be made to the relevant legislative or other document.

Principal Act

11   Until such time as a consolidating Act is produced, the Companies Act 1948 remains the principal Act, although it has been substantially amended by the Companies Acts 1967, 1976, 1980 and 1981. The main disclosure requirements for the preparation of accounts were originally set out in the eighth schedule to the 1948 Act. This schedule was revised by the 1967 Act, the second schedule of which became the new eighth schedule to the 1948 Act. The section 1(2) of the 1981 Act has now renumbered this schedule as schedule 8A to the 1948 Act, and its own first schedule has been inserted as a replacement eighth schedule to the 1948 Act. For ease of comprehension, this replacement eighth schedule is referred to throughout this book as the first schedule to the 1981 Act.

The Companies Acts 1948 to 1981

12   The Acts which together are cited as the Companies Acts 1948 to 1981 are:

(a)   The Companies Act 1948
(b)   The Companies Act 1967 (parts I and III)
(c)   The Companies (Floating Charges and Receivers) (Scotland) Act 1972*
(d)   The European Communities Act 1972 (section 9)*
(e)   The Stock Exchange (Completion of Bargains) Act 1976 (sections 1 to 4)*
(f)   The Insolvency Act 1976 (section 9)*
(g)   The Companies Act 1976*
(h)   The Companies Act 1980
(i)   The Companies Act 1981 (except sections 28 and 29)

However, the Acts marked * have no effect on company accounts disclosure.

Statutory Instruments

13   Statutory Instruments are from time to time issued to modify or supplement existing Companies Acts. References are made in the text to these Instruments where relevant.

Statements of Standard Accounting Practice

14   Statements of Standard Accounting Practice ('SSAPs') are prepared by the Accounting Standards Committee, and approved by the Councils of its

governing accountancy bodies. They contain both accounting policy and disclosure requirements. This book deals with SSAPs as they affect disclosure in accounts.

Stock Exchange Listing Agreement and the General Undertaking

15   There are additional disclosure requirements for companies listed on The Stock Exchange. These are set out in The Stock Exchange Listing Agreement (contained in The Stock Exchange publication *Admission of Securities to Listing*, which is generally known as the *Yellow Book*). Companies are required to enter into this agreement on their admission to listing, and to renew their agreement when any amendment is made to the standard form of the agreement. Similarly, companies whose shares are dealt with on the Unlisted Securities Market ('USM') are required to adopt the 'General Undertaking' set out in the publication *The Stock Exchange Unlisted Securities Market* (the *Green Book*). The additional disclosures required by the General Undertaking are very similar to those of the Listing Agreement. The requirements in this book referenced to the Listing Agreement should be taken to apply to USM companies, unless otherwise indicated.

Accounting Principles and Rules

16   The Companies Act 1981 has laid down several accounting principles and rules which a company must adopt in the preparation of its accounts. These rules are of two types — the 'historical cost accounting rules' and the 'alternative accounting rules'. The latter must be used if the main accounts are prepared on a current cost basis or, alternatively, if the main historical cost accounts incorporate the revaluation of any assets. We have included the historical cost rules in the disclosure requirements chapters, under relevant headings. The requirements set out in these chapters must be followed by companies in preparing their main accounts whether these are prepared on an historical cost or a current cost basis. The relevant additional requirements relating to the alternative accounting rules are set out in Chapter 9.

Banking, Insurance and Shipping Companies

17   Historically banking, insurance and shipping companies have enjoyed certain exemptions from disclosure under the Companies Acts. The accounts of banking and insurance companies are also subject to special rules in many other countries. The EEC Fourth Directive does not require member states to apply its provisions to banking and insurance companies, or to shipping companies before 1988. There are plans to issue parallel directives for the

contents of the annual accounts of banking and insurance companies, but these are still at an early stage.

18   The UK government has taken advantage of this exemption, in the following terms:

(a)   Companies subject to the exemption have the option to prepare their accounts under either the new rules or the old rules.

(b)   Any holding company that has a subsidiary that is an exempted company also has the option of preparing its group accounts according to either the new rules or the old rules.

'The new rules' mean:
  (i)   the new section 149 of the 1948 Act (introduced by section 1 of the 1981 Act);
 (ii)   the new section 152 of the 1948 Act (introduced by section 2 of the 1981 Act);
(iii)   the new schedule 8 to the 1948 Act (introduced by schedule 1 to the 1981 Act).

'The old rules' mean:
 (iv)   the original section 149 of the 1948 Act (now known as section 149A);
  (v)   the original section 152 of the 1948 Act (now known as section 152A);
 (vi)   schedule 8 to the 1948 Act as it existed prior to the 1981 Act (now known as schedule 8A).

19   The following restrictions should be noted:

(a)   A non-exempt holding company that has an exempt subsidiary, although it has the option in respect of its group accounts, must prepare its own accounts in accordance with the new rules.

(b)   Not all banking, insurance and shipping companies are exempted. Each term has a restricted meaning as follows:
  (i)   'Banking company' means a company which is recognised as a bank for the purposes of the Banking Act 1979, or is a licensed institution within the meaning of that Act.
 (ii)   'Insurance company' means a company to which part II of the Insurance Companies Act 1974 applies. In practice this can be taken to include all British insurance companies.
(iii)   'Shipping companies' are confined to those owning, operating or managing ships, and that satisfy the Secretary of State that they ought in the national interest to be treated for these purposes as shipping companies. Only a few shipping companies are in this position.

Introduction

Banking, insurance and shipping companies that take advantage of the option to continue to prepare their accounts under the old rules are in some cases permitted further disclosure exemptions within those old rules.

Investment Companies

20   Investment companies (as defined by paragraph 73 of the first schedule to the 1981 Act) are outside the scope of this book. The special requirements for such companies are set out in part V of the first schedule to the Companies Act 1981, in paragraph 10 of the Listing Agreement, and in Chapter 9 of the *Admission of Securities to Listing.*

Abbreviations and References

21   The following abbreviations are used throughout this book:

1948	s	
1967	s	
1976	s	Companies Acts, section reference
1980	s	
1981	s	
1981	1 sch	First schedule to the Companies Act 1981
SSAP		Statement of Standard Accounting Practice
SI		Statutory Instrument
LA		The Stock Exchange Listing Agreement
ASL		The Admission of Securities to Listing
USM		The Stock Exchange Unlisted Securities Market
Author		Additional comments or suggested treatment in the absence of legal or similar requirements.

Paragraphs dealing with specific items in the standard balance sheets have been referenced to format 2 (see Appendix 1).

2 Directors' Report

General

1. A directors' report must be attached to the balance sheet included in the annual statutory accounts.

   1948 s 157(1)

2. Reference is made throughout this chapter to the directors' report accompanying group accounts. If a company has no subsidiaries, references to the 'group' should be construed as applying to the company.

Principal Activities

3. The principal activities of the group during the year, and significant changes in such activities during the year, must be disclosed.

   1967 s 16(1)

Business Review

4. The report must contain a fair review of the development of the business of the group during the year, and of its position at the year end.

   1948 s 157(1)
   (introduced by 1981 s 13(1))

5. The Companies Act 1981 gives no guidance as to what constitutes a fair review. The intent of the EEC Fourth Directive is understood to be that the directors' report should include a commentary on the results such as is found in many European companies' accounts, and which in the United Kingdom is often found in the chairman's statement. However, the requirement in the Companies Act 1981 for a fair review need not be construed as requiring a long and detailed report and, until such time as the intent of this legislation is clarified, it should be assumed that a brief review of the results and position at the end of the year, with comments concerning any material developments in the business, will be adequate.

Material Differences from Published Forecasts

6. The directors' report should contain an explanation in the event that the trading results shown by the accounts differ materially from any published forecast made by the (holding) company.

   LA para 10(b)

Future Developments

7   An indication of likely future developments in the business of the group must be given.

1967 s 16(1)(f)(ii) (introduced by 1981 s 13(3))

8   In interpreting this requirement, directors should consider for disclosure major changes in activities which are planned or clearly envisaged. The legal provision is not considered to be a requirement to produce a forecast.

Dividends

9   The dividend recommended by the directors, and any amounts proposed to be carried to reserves, must be disclosed.

1948 s 157(1)

Significant Changes in Fixed Assets

10   The nature of significant changes in the fixed assets of the group during the year must be stated.

1967 s 16(1)(a)

Differences Between Market Value and Book Value of Land

11   Substantial differences between the market and book values of interests in land held as a fixed asset by the group must be indicated as precisely as practicable if, in the opinion of the directors, they are of such significance as to require them to be drawn to the attention of the members or debenture holders. Interests in land include the buildings thereon.

1967 s 16(1)(a)

12   It is recommended that where there are several interests in land, the aggregate market value and the aggregate book value should be compared to see if the difference is 'substantial'. When it is considered that a substantial difference exists, the basis on which the market value has been arrived at should be stated and consideration given to what reference, if any, should be made to taxation, including, where appropriate, development land tax and capital gains tax, payable on sale at a price equal to the estimated market value. An independent professional valuation is not required if the directors are competent to arrive at the 'market value' themselves, but the wording should make the position clear in this respect. Where property is situated in territories overseas, especially those subject to political unrest or where the remittance of currencies is restricted, it may not always be practicable, and may be misleading, to give the information required, and in such cases the wording should make this clear.

Post Balance Sheet Events

13   Particulars of important events which have occurred between the end of the financial year and the date of approval of the accounts, and which affect the company or any of its subsidiaries, must be disclosed. This requirement gives rise to two potential conflicts between the law and SSAP 17:

    (a)   SSAP 17:23 envisages disclosure only of non-adjusting events (and the reversal of window-dressing transactions), whereas the Act does not differentiate and thus must be construed as requiring disclosure of post balance sheet events whether adjusting or non-adjusting.

    (b)   The Act specifies disclosure in the directors' report whereas SSAP 17 envisages disclosure in the accounts.

1967 s 16(1)(f)(i) (introduced by 1981 s 13(3)) Author

14   Regarding (a) above, the financial effect of adjusting post balance sheet events, if particularly significant by reason of size or nature, would be disclosed in the accounts as exceptional or extraordinary items (see Chapter 6) in accordance with the requirements of SSAP 6. It is considered that such disclosure or its absence is a fair measure of whether the post balance sheet even is 'important' and thus falls to be disclosed in the directors' report. If this test of importance is met, it is suggested that the legal disclosure requirement would be observed by a brief mention in the directors' report together with reference to the relevant note to the accounts.

15   Regarding (b), many companies will not wish to make the disclosure twice over or partly in one place and partly in another. It is suggested that in view of the legal requirement, and because in any case the directors' report may be considered a more prominent disclosure medium than the accounts, the directors' report will be the appropriate place for disclosing non-adjusting post balance sheet events.

16   Where disclosure of non-adjusting events is made in the directors' report, the additional information required by SSAP 17 will need to be given, *viz*:

SSAP 17:24–25

    (a)   the nature of the event;

    (b)   an estimate, before taking account of taxation, of its financial effect, or a statement that such an estimate is impracticable; and

    (c)   its taxation implications.

If the opposing view is taken, non-adjusting balance sheet events being disclosed in the accounts instead of the directors' report, reference to the relevant note should be made in the directors' report in order to comply with the legal requirement.

Author

17 The information required by the preceding paragraph should also be given in respect of the reversal or maturity after the year end of any transaction entered into before the year end, the substance of which was primarily to alter the appearance of the company's balance sheet, regardless of whether treated as an adjusting or non-adjusting event for accounts purposes.

SSAP 17:23(b)

Research and Development

18 An indication of the activities, if any, of the group in the field of research and development must be given.

1967 s 16(1)(f)(iii) (introduced by 1981 s 13(3))

Contributions for Political and Charitable Purposes

19 The separate totals of contributions for political and charitable purposes made by the company (not being a wholly owned subsidiary of a company incorporated in Great Britain) or by the group, if together they exceed £200, must be disclosed. The name of the recipient must be given in the case of individual political contributions exceeding £200. Donations for political or charitable purposes made to persons (or parties) outside the United Kingdom are exempt.

1967 s 19
SI 1980 No 1055

Disabled Persons

20 If the average number of UK employees of the company during the year exceeded 250, the directors' report must state the company's policies for:

SI 1980 No 1160

(a) the employment of disabled persons;

(b) the continued employment and training of persons who become disabled whilst employed by the company; and

(c) the training, career development and promotion of disabled persons.

Health and Safety at Work

21 The Secretary of State may require any class of company to disclose specified information in the directors' report relating to the health, safety and welfare at work of its employees. No orders have yet been made under this provision.

1967 s 16(1)(g)

Directors and Service Contracts

22 The names of the (holding) company's directors, including the names of any persons who were directors at any time during the financial year, are to be disclosed. The directors' report for a listed company must further state the

1967 s 16(1)

LA para 11(d)

unexpired period of any service contract of any director proposed for reelection at the forthcoming annual general meeting. (This further provision does not apply to USM companies.)   USM 8:4

Directors' Interests in Shares or Debentures

23   Directors' interests in the shares or debentures of any group company (specifying the company concerned) together with corresponding details at the beginning of the financial year (or date of first appointment as director if later) must be disclosed, either in the directors' report or in a note to the accounts.   1967 s 16(1)(e), (4)
1967 s 16(4A)
(introduced by 1981 s ·13(4))

24   The above details (there are no exceptions on grounds of immateriality), must be given for each director and where no shares are held by a director this fact must be stated. The information is to be taken from the Register of Directors' Shareholdings and must include the interests of spouses and infant children. These details need not be given: 1967 s 16(1)(e)
1967 s 27, 31

(a)   in accounts of a wholly owned subsidiary where a person is a director of both a subsidiary and its holding company;   SI 1968 No 1533

(b)   in accounts of a wholly owned subsidiary of a company incorporated outside Great Britain;   SI 1968 No 1533

(c)   in relation to interests in a society registered under the Industrial and Provident Societies Act 1965;   SI 1968 No 865

(d)   in respect of certain trustee shareholdings.   SI 1967 No 1594
SI 1968 No 865

25   For listed companies, directors' interests in shares and debentures of the company and each of its subsidiaries (as required to be disclosed by the Companies Act 1967) should be distinguished between beneficial and other interests. (It may be appropriate for all companies to adopt this disclosure.) Particulars should be given as at the balance sheet date, but changes between that date and a date not more than one month prior to the date of the notice of the general meeting held to consider the accounts are to be shown as a note. If there are no changes, that fact should be disclosed.   LA para 10(h)

Author
LA para 10(h)

Waivers of Dividends

26   For listed companies, particulars of any arrangements under which any shareholder has waived or agreed to waive any dividends should be disclosed.   LA para 10(n)

Substantial Holdings

27   A statement should be given of persons (other than directors) holding or beneficially interested in any substantial part of the share capital of a listed company, disclosing the amounts of the holdings in question at a date not more than one month prior to the date of notice of meeting. If appropriate, a negative statement is to be given. A substantial shareholding is one which amounts to 5 per cent or more of any class of capital having full voting rights. Holdings by different companies in a group are counted as one for this purpose.

    LA para 10(i)

28   USM companies need only disclose the above information insofar as it is known to the directors. This information will, in practice, be available to the directors of USM companies by virtue of section 58 of the 1981 Act, which requires the holders of substantial interests in the equity capital of a public company to notify the company.

    USM 8:4

Company's Interest in its Own Shares

29   Where shares in the company:

    1967 s 16A(1)
    (introduced by 1981 s 14)

    (a)   are purchased by the company or acquired by forfeiture or by surrender in lieu of forfeiture; or

    (b)   are acquired by the company's nominee or any other person with financial assistance from the company and in a situation where the company has a beneficial interest in the shares; or

    (c)   are subject to a lien or other charge taken by the company;

the following information must be disclosed:

    1967 s 16A(2)
    (introduced by 1981 s 14)

    (i)   The number and nominal value of the shares purchased during the year, the consideration given, and the reasons for their purchase.

    (ii)   The number and nominal values of the shares so acquired or charged.

    (iii)   The maximum number and nominal value of the shares acquired or charged held during the year.

    (iv)   The number and nominal value of the shares acquired or charged which were disposed of or cancelled during the year.

    (v)   The percentages of the called up share capital represented by the shares disclosed in (i) to (iv) above.

    (vi)   The amount of the charge on any of the shares concerned.

    (vii)   The consideration for any such shares disposed of.

Close Company Status

30   For listed companies a statement should be made as to whether or not the close company provisions of the Income and Corporation Taxes Act 1970 (as amended) apply to the holding company and whether there has been any change since the end of the financial year. Where there is doubt, the existence of the doubt and basis on which taxation provisions have been made is to be noted. It is regarded as good practice for all companies to make this disclosure, whether listed or not.

LA para 10(j)

Author

Reappointment of Auditors

31   It is customary to include a statement at the foot of the directors' report stating what resolution will be put to the general meeting regarding the appointment or reappointment of the auditors.

Auditors' Responsibility

32   In preparing their report on the accounts, the auditors are required to consider whether in their opinion the information in the directors' report is consistent with the accounts, and if not they are required to say so. Auditors are not otherwise required to give an opinion on the directors' report.

1967 s 23A
(introduced by 1981 s 15)

3 Format

Introduction

1 Section 149(1) of the Companies Act 1948 (as introduced by section 1 of the Companies Act 1981) introduces the requirement for accounts to be prepared in a standard format. A choice of formats is permitted and these formats are set out in full in Appendix 1.

2 Two balance sheet formats are permitted. They generally specify the same main headings and differ principally in using in one case a vertical format and in the other a horizontal format.

3 Four profit and loss account formats are permitted. These consist of two alternative approaches, either of which may be adopted in a vertical or horizontal format. The principal difference between these approaches is in the classification of expense items. Formats 1 and 3 analyse expenses by function, and so disclose cost of sales, distribution costs and administrative expenses. Formats 2 and 4 analyse expenses by nature, showing raw materials purchased, staff costs, depreciation and other charges.

4 There is therefore a conceptual difference between the cost of sales figures derived from the alternative approaches. Formats 2 and 4 disclose less information about gross margins than formats 1 and 3, and this may be beneficial to manufacturing companies.

Compliance with Rules for Formats

5 All items in the standard formats are prefixed with a letter, a Roman numeral or an Arabic numeral. These indicate respectively headings, subheadings and detail.

6 Every balance sheet and profit and loss account of a company must show the items listed in one of the standard formats unless the special nature of the company's business justifies adaptation of those formats. Such adaptation is limited to rearrangement of the detail marked in the standard formats with an Arabic numeral. The letters and numbers used for identification purposes in the formats need not be written into the accounts.   1981 1 sch 1, 3(3)

14

7   Items listed in the standard formats and prefixed with a letter or a Roman numeral must be included in the accounts in the same order and under the same headings and subheadings as in the standard format chosen.

        1981 1 sch 1(1)

8   Headings in the standard formats should not be abbreviated, even if the heading is not wholly appropriate to the items included thereunder. For example, 'Bank loans and overdrafts' should not be abbreviated to 'Bank loans' where a company has bank loans but no overdrafts.

9   Once a standard format has been chosen, it must be adopted consistently in future years unless, in the opinion of the directors, there are special reasons for a change, in which case details of the change and the reasons for it must be given in a note to the accounts. In the year in which the formats are first adopted, a company will not be required to give details of the change from the layout previously adopted. However, most companies will wish to provide some explanation as to the reason why they have changed the presentation of their accounts.

        1981 1 sch 2(1)

        1981 1 sch 2(2)
Author

10   Any item required to be shown in the chosen standard format may be shown in greater detail e.g. subanalysed, if desired.

        1981 1 sch 3(1)

11   Additional items may be included, if not covered by an item in the standard formats.

        1981 1 sch 3(2)

12   Items indicated by an Arabic numeral in the standard formats may be combined in the balance sheet or profit and loss account, with the individual items shown instead in the notes, if such combination aids comprehension of the accounts.

        1981 1 sch 3(4)(b)

13   Corresponding amounts for the previous financial year must be shown for every item in the balance sheet, profit and loss account, and notes to the accounts, except in those cases specifically mentioned in this book.

        1981 1 sch 4(1), 58(2)

14   Where a corresponding amount would not be comparable with the current year item, an adjusted corresponding amount must be shown, particulars of the adjustment and the reasons for it being included in a note.

        1981 1 sch 4(2)

15   The netting off of assets and liabilities or income and expenditure is not permitted. This does not preclude the aggregation of debtor and creditor balances with the same party, so as to arrive at a net indebtedness. The full amounts of bank loans and overdrafts should be shown unless there is a legal right of set off, in which case these accounts should be netted off and the resultant balance shown as item C IV or C 2 as appropriate.

        1981 1 sch 5
Author

Flexibility

16   The use of standard formats may seem inflexible and likely to hinder the preparation of accounts in a form best suited to a specific company's business. However, the overriding consideration is that a true and fair view must be given. Directors are therefore required to:

    (a)   provide additional information not required by the standard formats or disclosure rules where failure to do so would prevent a true and fair view from being given; and

    (b)   depart from the standard formats or disclosure rules where, owing to special circumstances, compliance would prevent a true and fair view from being given.

    If the directors apply subparagraph (b) above, then they are to give details of, reasons for, and the effects of such departures.

Author

1948 s 149(2)–(4) (introduced by 1981 s 1(1))

17   A heading must be omitted from the specified formats where there is a nil balance for both the current and preceding financial years.

1981 1 sch 3(5), 4(3)

18   The amount of any item indicated by an Arabic number, if immaterial, may be included under another heading within the format. In such circumstances, disclosure in the notes is not required.

1981 1 sch 3(4)(a)
Author

19   The disclosure requirements of the first schedule to the Companies Act 1981 may be disregarded in respect of any amounts which are considered immaterial. This dispensation does not apply to disclosure requirements elsewhere in the 1981 Act, or introduced by other legislation.

1981 1 sch 85

20   Unless otherwise indicated in this book, the disclosures required in addition to those of the standard formats may be made either on the face of the accounts or in the notes.

4 Accounting Principles and Policies

General

1   The Companies Act 1981 sets out, for the first time in statute, accounting principles which must be followed in the statutory accounts, whether these are prepared on an historical or current cost basis. The accounting principles follow closely the fundamental accounting concepts mentioned in SSAP 2.   *1981 1 sch 9*

Accounting Principles

2   The Companies Act 1981 has specified four fundamental accounting principles which must be applied, and these are as follows:

(a)   The company shall be presumed to be carrying on its business as a going concern.   *1981 1 sch 10 SSAP 2:14(a), 17*

(b)   Accounting policies must be applied consistently from one financial year to the next.   *1981 1 sch 11 SSAP 2:14(c)*

(c)   All items must be determined on a prudent basis, and in particular:-   *1981 1 sch 12 SSAP 2:14(d)*
     (i)   revenue and profits must not be anticipated, but should be recognised by inclusion in the profit and loss account only when realised in the form of cash or of other assets the ultimate realisation of which can be assessed with reasonable certainty; and
     (ii)   all liabilities and losses which have arisen or are likely to arise in respect of the financial year to which the accounts relate or a previous financial year must be taken into account, including those which only become apparent between the balance sheet date and the date on which the balance sheet is signed.   *SSAP 2:14(d) SSAP 17:19, 22*

(d)   All income and charges relating to the financial year covered by the accounts must be taken into account without regard to the date of receipt or payment. This is commonly referred to as the 'accruals' concept.   *1981 1 sch 13 SSAP 2:14(b)*

3   In determining the aggregate amount of any item in a company's balance   1981 1 sch 14
     sheet or profit and loss account, the amount of each individual asset or
     liability included in that amount shall be determined separately. For
     example, in calculating the amount at which stocks are to be stated, the test   Author
     'lower of cost and net realisable value' is to be applied to each individual
     stock line, rather than to the total stock holding.

4   If the directors consider that there are special reasons for departing from any   1981 1 sch 15
     of the principles set out above they may do so, provided that particulars of   SSAP 2:17
     the departure, the reasons for it, and its effect are stated in a note to the
     accounts.

Accounting Rules

5   The first schedule of the 1981 Act distinguishes two sets of accounting rules,   1981 1 sch 16–34
     known respectively as the historical cost accounting rules and the alternative
     accounting rules. Whichever set of accounting rules is adopted, the   1981 1 sch 9
     accounting principles set out above remain of general application.

Accounting Policies

6   The accounting policies adopted in determining the amounts to be included   1981 1 sch 36
     in respect of all material items shown in the balance sheet and in determining   SSAP 2:18
     the profit or loss must be stated in a note to the accounts. In particular the
     1981 Act requires the policies followed in respect of the following matters to
     be explained:

     (a)   Foreign currency translation.   1981 1 sch 58(1)
                                             SSAP 6:6
     (b)   Depreciation and diminution in value of assets.   1981 1 sch 36
                                                              SSAP 12:22

7   Additionally, various SSAPs require the adoption and disclosure of
     accounting policies in respect of certain other items not specifically covered
     by the Act. These are dealt with in this book under the relevant headings. As
     noted in paragraph 2 of the Explanatory Foreword to Statements of
     Standard Accounting Practice, and as required by paragraph 10(a) of the
     Listing Agreement, explanation should be made in the accounts for any
     significant departure from an SSAP.

Assets other than goodwill arising on consolidation

8   The following accounting policies apply to all items described in the balance

sheet as fixed assets (other than goodwill arising on consolidation) and therefore relate to intangibles, tangibles and also fixed asset investments.

Cost

9 Where any fixed assets are included other than at historical cost (i.e. on a revalued or current cost basis), reference should be made to the alternative accounting rules set out in Chapter 9.

10 Subject to any provision for depreciation, the amount to be included in respect of any fixed asset must be its purchase price or production cost. Such purchase price or production cost must be determined according to the following rules: 1981 1 sch 17

 (a) Purchase price must include the incidental costs of acquisition. 1981 1 sch 26(1)

 (b) Production cost must include the purchase price of raw materials and consumables used, together with the other costs incurred which may be directly attributable to the production of the asset. 1981 1 sch 26(2)

 (c) Production cost may include a reasonable proportion of the costs incurred by the company which are only indirectly attributable to the production of that asset, but only to the extent that they relate to the period of production. 1981 1 sch 26(3)(a)

 (d) Production cost may include interest on capital borrowed to finance the acquisition of that asset, to the extent that it accrues in respect of the period of production. Interest so included is to be disclosed in a note to the accounts. 1981 1 sch 26(3)(b)

11 Government grants, unless treated as a deferred credit, should be deducted from the cost of the fixed assets to which the grants relate. SSAP 4:9

12 Where no record of the purchase price or production cost of an asset exists, or such record cannot be obtained without unreasonable expense or delay, the purchase price or production cost shall be the value of the asset according to the earliest available record of its value. Where advantage is taken of this rule for the first time, particulars must be given in a note to the accounts. 1981 1 sch 28, 51(1)

13 Where the amount repayable on a debt exceeds the value of consideration received (e.g. redemption of a loan issued at a discount), the difference may be treated as an 'asset', which must be written off by reasonable amounts each year, and be completely written off prior to repayment of the debt. If the unamortised amount is not shown in the balance sheet as a separate item, it must be disclosed in a note to the accounts. It is not clear where such an item 1981 1 sch 24

  Author

would be presented in the balance sheet formats. It may be appropriate to introduce a new line, C II 7, insofar as the item is in the nature of a prepayment.

Depreciation

14 Fixed assets having a limited useful economic life are to be depreciated to their residual values, if any, systematically over such life. However, it should be noted that SSAP 19 states that certain investment properties should not be amortised in this way. The consequences of this recommendation are discussed in Chapter 9.

1981 1 sch 18
SSAP 12:16–17
SSAP 19:10

15 The unamortised cost of fixed assets should be written off over the remaining useful life where there is either:

(a) a revision of the estimated useful life; or
(b) a change in the method of depreciation.

SSAP 12:18
SSAP12:20

16 Any fixed asset (including an investment) whose value is considered to have diminished permanently must be written down to its estimated recoverable amount, which if necessary should then be amortised over its remaining useful life.

1981 1 sch 19(2)
SSAP 12:19

17 Fixed asset investments may, however, be written down where there has been diminution in value even if that diminution is not considered to be permanent. The law is permissive rather than prescriptive on this point. Such a write down may be prudent, but would not be regarded as normal practice.

1981 1 sch 19(1)

Author

18 Fixed assets written down as above must be restored (wholly or partly as appropriate) to their original value, where the reasons for making the write down have ceased to apply.

1981 1 sch 19(3)

Goodwill

19 Goodwill acquired by a company for valuable consideration must be treated as a fixed asset, in accordance with the rules set out above, and must therefore be written off over a period not exceeding its 'useful economic life'. However, goodwill arising upon consolidation is not required by law to be amortised. It is therefore desirable that companies should clearly explain the accounting policies adopted in respect of goodwill, and especially so in the case of balance sheets containing both purchased goodwill and goodwill arising on consolidation.

1981 1 sch 21

1981 1 sch 66

Author

Current assets

20 Subject to the proviso in the following paragraph, the amount to be included in respect of any current asset must be its purchase price or production cost determined in the same way as for a fixed asset. These concepts will normally only be relevant to stocks and investments.

1981 1 sch 22

Author

21	Where the net realisable value of any current asset is lower than the purchase price or production cost, it must be included at net realisable value.	1981 1 sch 23(1)
22	Where a current asset has been written down to net realisable value in accordance with the preceding paragraph, the asset must be restored (wholly or partly as appropriate) to its original value if the reasons for writing it down cease to apply.	1981 1 sch 23(2)
23	Distribution costs must not be included in production costs for any current asset.	1981 1 sch 26(4)
24	Any stocks or fungible assets (see below) included at purchase price or production cost may be determined by any one of the following methods:	1981 1 sch 27

(a) FIFO (first in, first out).

(b) LIFO (last in, first out).

(c) Weighted average.

(d) Other methods similar to (a), (b) or (c).

25	Although the law allows the adoption of LIFO, SSAP 9 discourages its use. In any case the method of determining cost must be one which appears to the directors to be appropriate in the circumstances of the company.	SSAP 9: Appendix 1:12 1981 1 sch 27(1)
26	Fungible assets are assets which are substantially indistinguishable from other assets included in the same category. These will include investments (see Chapter 5).	1981 1 sch 27(6)

5 Balance Sheet

Format

1   The rules governing the selection and adaptation of the alternative formats are set out in Chapter 3 of this book. In the following paragraphs, items are dealt with in the order in which they arise in balance sheet format 2, and references to 'item...' in the following paragraphs are to that format.

Group Companies

2   If a company is a member of a group of companies, in the case of every item where the balance sheet formats require the disclosure of the balance attributable to group companies (*viz* investments, debtors and creditors) there must be a further analysis between: 1981 1 sch 59

(a)   amounts attributable to the company's holding company and fellow subsidiaries; and

(b)   amounts attributable to the company's subsidiaries.

There is an equivalent provision, in relation to the consolidated accounts, with respect to balances attributable to unconsolidated subsidiaries.   1981 1 sch 67

Modified Accounts

3   Companies preparing 'modified accounts' should refer to Chapter 10, which explains how the rules set out in this chapter are to be applied to the modified accounts.

Fixed Assets (Item B)

Definition

4   Fixed assets are assets intended for use on a continuing basis in the company's activities. Other assets must be taken to be current assets.   1981 1 sch 75

General

5   Fixed assets must be shown subdivided into three groups: 1981 1 sch formats

(a)   Intangible assets.
(b)   Tangible assets.
(c)   Investments.

6   In respect of each item shown as a 'fixed asset' in the standard format there   1981 1 sch 42(1)–(2)
must be stated:

(a)   the amount of that item stated at cost (or, where the alternative
accounting rules are used, at a revaluation or current cost) at the
beginning and end of the financial year; and

(b)   the effect on that item of:
(i)   acquisitions during the year;
(ii)   disposals during the year;
(iii) transfers of assets of the company to and from that item during the
year;
(iv)   any revision of the amount of that item during the year as a result
of that item being valued on an acceptable accounting basis other
than cost.

7   In respect of each item shown above, there must also be stated the amounts   1981 1 sch 42(3)
of:

(a)   the accumulated depreciation at the beginning and end of the financial
year;

(b)   any provisions for depreciation or diminution in value made in the
financial year;

(c)   any adjustments to such provisions resulting from the disposal of any
assets during the financial year; and

(d)   any other adjustments made to such provisions during the year.

8   Corresponding amounts for the previous year are not required for the   1981 1 sch 58(3)
reconciliations in the preceding two paragraphs.

9   In addition SSAP 12 requires, for all fixed assets subject to depreciation, the   SSAP 12:22
disclosure of:

    (a)   the depreciation method(s) used;

    (b)   the useful lives or the depreciation rates used;

    (c)   the effect, if material, on depreciation in the year of:
       (i)   a change in the method of depreciation;   SSAP 12:19
      (ii)   a revaluation of fixed assets.   SSAP 12:20

10   Where any fixed assets are valued on a basis other than cost, the alternative   1981 1 sch 29–34
accounting rules, which require additional disclosures, will apply (see
Chapter 9). In particular, these rules will apply to historical cost accounts
including land and buildings at a revalued amount.

11   Where interest on capital borrowed to finance the production of an asset has   1981 1 sch 26(3)(b)
been included in the production cost of that asset, that fact must be disclosed
together with the amount of interest so included. In addition, listed   LA para 10(g)
companies should state the amount and treatment of any related tax relief.

12   Although it is not clear whether the amount of such interest should be
disclosed only in the year in which it is first capitalised, or in all subsequent
years in which the asset is carried in the accounts, the former course will
normally be appropriate.

Intangible fixed assets (item B I)
Development costs (item B I 1)

13   Although pure and applied research expenditure must be written off as   1981 1 sch 3(2)(c)
incurred, development costs may be included in a company's balance sheet in   SSAP 13:20–21
special circumstances. In such cases there must be stated in a note to the   1981 1 sch 20
accounts:

    (a)   the reasons for capitalising the expenditure; and
    (b)   the period over which the costs are being written off.

     SSAP 13 sets out the criteria for determining such 'special circumstances'.   SSAP 13:15–16, 21
Expenditure incurred in locating and exploiting mineral deposits in the
extractive industries is specifically excluded from the scope of the standard.

14   The accounting policy followed for research and development expenditure   SSAP 13:29
should be clearly explained.

15   Development expenses are to be treated as a realised loss in computing   1980 s 42A
distributable profits, even if carried forward, unless the directors consider   (introduced by 1981 s 84)
that there are special circumstances (see above) for not so treating them.
Such reasons must be disclosed in a note to the accounts.

Concessions, patents, licences, trade marks etc (item B I 2)

16   Trade marks, patents and similar rights and assets must not be included in a balance sheet unless:

    (a)   the assets were acquired for valuable consideration, and are not required to be shown as goodwill; or

    (b)   the assets in question were created by the company itself.

    The patent costs to be included under the balance sheet heading should exclude any associated development expenditure.

1981 1 sch format note 2

Author

Goodwill (item B I 3)

17   The following statutory provisions do not deal with goodwill arising upon consolidation.

1981 1 sch 66

18   Amounts representing goodwill can only be included to the extent that the goodwill was acquired for valuable consideration.

1981 1 sch format note 3

19   Such goodwill must be depreciated systematically over a period chosen by the directors of the company, which must not exceed (but by implication may be less than) its useful economic life. This provision therefore allows goodwill to be written off when it is purchased. In such circumstances, the goodwill need not be included in the reconciliations required for fixed assets.

1981 1 sch 21(1)–(3)

Author

20   The reasons for choosing the period over which the goodwill is written off, and the period chosen, must be disclosed in a note to the accounts.

1981 1 sch 21(4)

21   There is much debate as to what represents the useful economic life of goodwill. No relevant accounting standard has yet been issued by the Accounting Standards Committee. However, the American accounting profession has set a maximum life of 40 years.

Tangible fixed assets (item B II)

22   Tangible fixed assets include land and buildings, plant and machinery, fixtures, fittings, tools and equipment, payments on account and assets under construction. The general rules regarding fixed assets have been set out above. Certain specific rules are set out below.

Land and buildings (item B II 1)

23   In relation to amounts shown as 'land and buildings':

1981 1 sch 44

    (a)   the amounts included as freehold and leasehold land must be disclosed separately; and

   (b)   an analysis of leasehold land between long and short leases must be
         given.

24   Long leases are those for which the unexpired term at the balance sheet date   1981 1 sch 82
     is not less than 50 years, and short leases are all other leases.

Investment properties

25   An investment property is defined as an interest in land and/or buildings: SSAP 19:7

   (a)   in respect of which construction and development have been completed;
         and

   (b)   which is held for its investment potential, with any rental income being
         negotiated at arm's length.

     However, a property owned by a company and either occupied by it for its   SSAP 19:8
     own purposes, or let to another group company, is not to be treated as an
     investment property.

26   Investment properties should be carried in the balance sheet at open market   SSAP 19:11, 15
     value, and that carrying value should be prominently displayed. This   Author
     requirement will be satisfied by showing investment properties separately in
     the analysis of fixed assets given in the notes. Carrying investment properties
     at market value will automatically bring the company within the scope of the
     alternative accounting rules (see Chapter 9).

27   The names of the valuers, or particulars of their qualifications, must be   1981 1 sch 43
     disclosed together with the bases of valuation used by them. If a valuer is an   SSAP 19:12
     employee or officer of the company or group, that fact should also be stated.

Other tangible fixed assets

28   Tangible fixed assets of a kind which are constantly being replaced (e.g.   1981 1 sch 25(1)–(2)
     moulds and dies or hotel furnishings) may be included at a fixed quantity
     and value where their overall value is not material to assessing the company's
     state of affairs, and their quantity, value and composition are not subject to
     material variation.

Investments (item B III or C III)

General

29   Investments may be included in the balance sheet as either fixed or current
     assets. Investments in the nature of trade investments or other investments
     held on a long term basis should normally be treated as fixed, and
     investments of a temporary nature (e.g. investments representing the
     employment outside the business of temporarily surplus funds) should be
     treated as current assets.

30   Listed investments are those which have been granted a listing on a recognised stock exchange, or on any stock exchange of repute (other than a recognised stock exchange) outside Great Britain. The only recognised stock exchange is The Stock Exchange. For guidance as to whether or not a stock exchange outside Great Britain is 'reputable', The Stock Exchange should be consulted. Shares dealt in on the USM are not considered to be listed.

1981 1 sch 83

Author

31   For each item listed in the standard formats under investments (whether fixed or current) there must be stated the amount attributable to listed investments, and an analysis given differentiating between investments listed on a recognised stock exchange and those which have been granted a listing on other stock exchanges of repute.

1981 1 sch 45(1)

32   Notwithstanding that many overseas listed investments are also listed on The Stock Exchange, it would seem appropriate that investments should be analysed according to the location of the principal market in their shares.

33   For listed investments there must also be stated:

1981 1 sch 45(2)

(a)   the aggregate market value of those investments, where it differs from the amount at which they are included in the balance sheet; and

(b)   the market value and the stock exchange value, if for accounts purposes the former is taken as higher than the latter.

These provisions will apply to a holding company having a listed subsidiary. In such circumstances the stock exchange price may be an unrealistic measure of market value, since it will not contemplate a holding affording a controlling interest. If the directors feel that the market value exceeds the stock exchange value, disclosure must be made under (b) above, and it will be desirable for the notes to include an explanation of the reasons for the differing valuations.

Author

Fungible assets

34   Assets of any description are regarded as fungible if they are indistinguishable one from another. Such assets will normally only include stocks and investments. The following rules will usually only be relevant to investments because there are equivalent provisions (set out elsewhere in this chapter) which apply to all stocks, whether fungible or not.

1981 1 sch 27(6)

Author

35   Shares of a particular class which confer identical rights on the holder should be regarded as fungible, even though they are individually distinguishable by numbers.

| 36 | The cost of any fixed or current asset which is considered to be fungible may be determined by either the FIFO, LIFO, weighted average or any other similar method which matches sales with original cost on an estimated basis. | 1981 1 sch 27(1)–(2) |

| 37 | If there is a material difference between the value for accounts purposes of any fungible assets, whose cost is determined by one of the above methods, and its value at replacement cost or most recent purchase price or production cost (whichever the directors consider the more appropriate comparison) the amount of the difference must be stated in a note to the accounts. | 1981 1 sch 27(3)–(5) |

Own shares (item B III 7 or C III 2)

| 38 | The nominal value of any of its own shares held by a company and disclosed under one of the above headings must be shown separately. | 1981 1 sch format note 4 |

Subsidiary companies

| 39 | A company shall be deemed to be another's holding company if, but only if, that other is its subsidiary. | 1948 s 154(4) |

| 40 | A company (company S) shall be deemed to be a subsidiary of another company (company H) if, but only if: | 1948 s 154(1) |

    (a)   company H is a member of company S and controls, directly or indirectly, the composition of its board of directors; or

    (b)   company H, directly or indirectly, holds more than half in nominal value of its equity share capital; or

    (c)   company S is a subsidiary of any company which is company H's subsidiary.

| 41 | A company shall be deemed to be a fellow subsidiary of another company if both are subsidiaries of the same body corporate but neither is the other's subsidiary. | 1981 1 sch 79 |

| 42 | In respect of each subsidiary company the following information must be given in a note to the accounts. However, in the case of group accounts, the disclosures marked need only be made in relation to the holding company's accounts: | 1981 1 sch 63(d) |

    (a)   The subsidiary's name.   1967 s 3(1)

    (b)   The country of incorporation (if other than Great Britain) or country of registration (England or Scotland) if incorporated in Great Britain and not registered in the same country as the holding company.   1967 s 3(1)

    (c)   A description of the shares held and the proportion of the nominal value of the issued shares of each class held (distinguishing between shares   1967 s 3(1)(c), (2)   SSAP 14:33

held directly by the holding company and those held by another subsidiary). The corresponding amount for the previous year need not be stated.   1981 1 sch 58(3)

(d)   The aggregate capital and reserves at the most recent financial year end.   1981 s 4(3)(a)

(e)   The profit or loss for the most recent financial year.   1981 s 4(3)(b)

(f)   The nature of its business (if a principal subsidiary).   SSAP 14:33

(g)   In the case of a listed holding company, the principal country of operations of active material subsidiaries.   LA para 10(d)

43   The information in (d) and (e) of the preceding paragraph is not required if:

(a)   the company, being the wholly owned subsidiary of another company incorporated in Great Britain, is exempted from preparing group accounts; or   1981 s 4(4)

(b)   the company prepares group accounts; and: 1981 s 4(4)

  (i)   the accounts of the subsidiary are included in the group accounts; or

  (ii) the investment in the subsidiary is included in, or in a note to, the company's accounts by way of the equity method of accounting; or

(c)   the investment is included in, or in a note to, the company's accounts by way of the equity method of valuation; or   1981 s 4(5)

(d)   the company holds less than one half of the nominal value of the allotted share capital of the subsidiary, and the subsidiary is not required to file its balance sheet with the registrar and does not otherwise publish that balance sheet in Great Britain or elsewhere; or   1981 s 4(6)

(e)   the information is not material.   1981 s 4(7)

44   If the above disclosure requirements would, in the opinion of the directors of the holding company, result in particulars of excessive length being given, the information need only be given in respect of those subsidiaries which principally affect the amount of the profit or loss or the assets of the company and its subsidiaries. If this is done, the fact must be stated and the full particulars annexed to the next annual return.   1967 s 3(4)

1967 s 3(5)
1981 s 4(8)

45   With the consent of the Department of Trade, the information required to be given for subsidiary companies need not be given in respect of subsidiaries incorporated or carrying on business outside the United Kingdom, if in the opinion of the directors of the holding company this would be harmful to the business of the holding company or of any other company in the group, or of the subsidiary.   1967 s 3(3)

46   Where the company has subsidiaries whose accounts are not coterminous   1981 1 sch 70
with those of the holding company, there must be stated in relation to each
subsidiary in a note to the accounts (whether or not they are dealt with in any
group accounts):

(a)   the reasons why the company's directors consider that the subsidiaries'
financial years should not coincide with that of the company;

(b)   the dates at which the last preceding accounts of the subsidiaries were
closed, or the earliest and latest dates.

In respect of group accounts, SSAP 14 requires the names of the principal   SSAP 14:18
subsidiaries concerned to be stated and, if the length of a principal
subsidiary's accounting period differs from that of the holding company, the
period is to be stated. Full details are given in Chapter 8.

47   A subsidiary company must not hold shares in its holding company, unless   1948 s 27
those shares were acquired before 1 July 1948; any allotment or transfer of
shares in a holding company to its subsidiary is void. ('Holding company'
here means all companies of which the company in question is a subsidiary,
including intermediate holding companies.)

48   If a subsidiary holds, either directly or through nominees, shares of or   1981 1 sch 60
debentures in its holding company, the holding company must disclose in a
note to its accounts the number, description and amount of shares or
debentures so held. However disclosure is not required if the shares or
debentures are held either:

(a)   as personal representative; or

(b)   as trustee, and neither the company nor any subsidiary is beneficially
interested under the trust, otherwise than as security for transactions
entered into in the ordinary course of business.

Related companies (*item B III 3*)
49   The following paragraphs compare the accounting requirements introduced
by the 1981 Act for related companies with those of SSAP 1 for associated
companies. The disclosures required in respect of these investments are set
out later, under the heading 'Investment Disclosures'.

50   A 'related company' is defined as a non-group company in which an investor   1981 1 sch 91
company holds a long term 'qualifying capital interest' (i.e. an interest in
voting equity shares) for the purpose of securing a contribution to the
investor's own activities by the exercise of control or influence. Where the
equity stake exceeds 20 per cent, there is a presumption of such influence

unless the contrary is shown. If the stake exceeds 20 per cent and the company is not treated as related, its name and particulars of the investor's interest should be stated. SSAP 1:21

51   This definition is not identical to that of an associated company as set out in SSAP 1. However, the definitions do not differ in any material respect, and the distinction is unlikely to present many practical difficulties. This assumption will have to be reviewed when an accounting standard based on Exposure Draft 25 replaces SSAP 1, but it is likely that differences between the standard and the law will diminish rather than increase. In this book, associated and related companies have been treated as being the same.

52   The accounting requirements for the inclusion of interests in related companies in the consolidated balance sheet are as follows:

(a) SSAP 1 states that the group's interest should be at cost, less amounts written off, plus the group's share of the investee's post acquisition retained profits and reserves. SSAP 1:19

(b) The 1981 Act permits the equity method of accounting in consolidated accounts, in respect of investments that in the opinion of the directors are 'closely associated' with any company included in those consolidated accounts. This clearly includes related companies as defined in the Act; the Act is thus consistent with SSAP 1. 1981 1 sch 65(1)–(2)

53   SSAP 1 is not specific as to how the investment in related companies should be carried in the investing entity's own balance sheet. However, there is a requirement to show the investor's share of the investee's post acquisition retained profits and reserves by way of note. Carrying the investment on either of the following bases would comply with the standard: Author / SSAP 1:19 / Author

(a) At cost (less provision where required).
(b) At valuation.

It is clearly within the terms of the 1981 Act to carry the investment at cost. The legal authority for carrying the investment at valuation is twofold, as follows:

(c) The general 'alternative accounting rule' that fixed asset investments may be carried at valuation. 1981 1 sch 31(3)

(d) Reference to the 'equity method of valuation' (as opposed to the 'equity method of accounting') of investments in the context of the entity balance sheet. 1981 s 4(5)

The equity method of valuation is taken to mean a valuation method that arrives at the same balance sheet amount as would the equity method of accounting, but with changes in the year being passed through revaluation reserve rather than the profit and loss account.	Author

54   If a related company is not equity accounted in the consolidated accounts, the reasons should be stated. If the accounts of a related company are not coterminous with those of the investing company, or unaudited accounts are used, the facts and the accounting dates should be shown.   SSAP 1:11–12

55   The consolidated retained reserves are to be analysed, distinguishing between that part attributable to the group and that attributable to the related companies. The effect of any further tax on the distribution of the retained reserves of overseas related companies should be explained.   SSAP 1:20

Investment disclosures

56   The disclosure requirements for investments have been complicated by the various exemptions that have been granted, and the different information required for different levels of interest.

57   Subject to the exemptions mentioned in later paragraphs, further information must be disclosed (usually in the notes to the accounts) about investments in companies that are not subsidiary companies if the shareholdings fall into one or more of the following categories:

Category A The investee is not a subsidiary of the investor and either:

(a)   the shareholding exceeds one-tenth of the nominal share capital of any class of the investee's equity capital, or exceeds one-tenth but not one-fifth of its allotted share capital; or   1967 s 4(1)
   1967 s 4(1A)
   (introduced by 1981 s 3(1))

(b)   the amount of the shareholding as shown in the investing company's accounts exceeds one-tenth of the assets shown in its accounts. Assets should normally be taken to be 'gross' assets but there would seem to be no objection to net assets being used if more appropriate.   1967 s 4(2)
   Author

Category B The amount of the shareholding as shown in the investing company's accounts exceeds one-fifth of the nominal value of the allotted share capital of the investee company. (This will often mean that the investee is a related company.)   1981 s 4(2)

   Author

Category C The shareholding controlled either by the investor or by the investing group is such that the investee falls to be treated as a related company but is not within category A or B above. An example of an investment in this category would be the case of five group companies each   SSAP 1:6
   LA para 10(e)
   Author

having a 5 per cent interest in the investee. The group holding would be 25 per cent, and the investee would normally be a related company, although none of the holdings would be disclosed under categories A and B above.

58   The information to be disclosed about the investee company is set out in the following table — the disclosures for categories A and B need be made only in the accounts of the investor company, and not in group accounts. The disclosure for category C should, however, be made in group accounts.

                          1981 1 sch 63(b), (d), 68
                          Author

Investment category

	A	B	C
(a) Its name.	1967 s 4	1967 s 4	SSAP 1:21
(b) Its country of incorporation (if other than Great Britain).	1967 s 4	1967 s 4	
(c) Its country of registration (i.e. England or Scotland) if incorporated in Great Britain, when that country is not the same as the country of registration of the investing company.	1967 s 4	1967 s 4	
(d) Description and proportion of the nominal value of the issued shares of each class held. Comparative figures for the preceding year are not required by virtue of paragraph 58(3) of the first schedule to the 1981 Act.	1967 s 4	1967 s 4	SSAP 1:21
(e) The aggregate capital and reserves at the most recent financial year end.		1981 s 4(3) see 59 below	
(f) Its results for the most recent financial year.		1981 s 4(3) see 59 below	
(g) A summary of the tangible and intangible assets if required to give a fair understanding of the nature of the investment, if the investee company is treated as related.		SSAP 1:19	SSAP 1:19

If the investment exceeds 20 per cent of the investee's equity capital, the accounts of a listed company (or group) should also show:

(h) Its principal country of operations.		LA para 10(e)	
(i) Particulars of its issued share and loan capital and reserves, if not treated as a related company.	LA para 10(e)		

Balance Sheet

    (j)   Percentage of each class of loan capital attributable to the company's interest.   LA para 10(e)

59   However, the information otherwise required to be given for investments in category **B** by virtue of subparagraphs (e) and (f) above may be omitted if:

    (a)   the information is immaterial; or   1981 s 4(7)

    (b)   the investment is accounted for in the investor's own accounts by the equity method of valuation; or   1981 s 4(5)

    (c)   the investee company is not required to file its balance sheet with the registrar of companies and does not otherwise publish its balance sheet anywhere in the world, and the investment is less than 50 per cent of the nominal value of the allotted share capital of the investee company.   1981 s 4(6)

60   None of the above statutory investment disclosures need be made if in the opinion of the directors:

    (a)   the information required would be of excessive length. It may then be limited to those investments which principally affect the amount of the profit of loss or the assets of the group or investing company. In this event, the fact that only limited disclosure has been made must be stated in the accounts and the full particulars annexed to the next annual return; or   1967 s 4(4)

    (b)   disclosure would be harmful to the investor's business, or to that of the investee. This exemption is only available with the consent of the Department of Trade, and only in respect of investee companies incorporated or carrying on business outside the United Kingdom.   1967 s 4(3)

Debentures of the company

61   The nominal amount and book value of any debentures of the company held by a nominee or trustee for the company must be shown. Such debentures could conveniently be shown as other investments under item C III 3, and the details disclosed by note.   1981 1 sch 41(3) Author

Tax certificates of deposit

62   Tax certificates of deposit should be shown separately in the balance sheet, and will normally be treated as current assets and included as item C III 3.

Current Assets (Item C)

Stocks (item C I)

63 Total stocks and work in progress should be stated in the balance sheet at the lower of cost and net realisable value, and subclassified in a manner appropriate to the business, and so as to indicate the amounts held in each of the main categories. This will often be achieved by giving the analysis required, in any case, by the 1981 Act formats for the balance sheet.

1981 1 sch 23(1)
SSAP 9:26, 29

Author

64 Where differing bases have been adopted for valuing different types of stocks and work in progress, the amount included in the accounts under each basis should be stated.

SSAP 9:12

65 A suitable description of the amounts at which stocks and work in progress are stated in the accounts might be 'at the lower of cost and net realisable value' or, in the case of long term contract work in progress, 'at cost plus attributable profit (if any) less foreseeable losses (if any) and progress payments received and receivable', but the accounting policies which have been used in calculating cost, net realisable value, attributable profit and foreseeable losses (as appropriate) should also be stated.

SSAP 9:11

SSAP 9:28

66 The purchase price or production cost of stocks may be determined by whichever of the following bases appears appropriate to the directors:

1981 1 sch 27(1)–(2)

(a) FIFO (first in, first out).
(b) LIFO (last in, first out).
(c) Weighted average method.
(d) Other methods similar to (a), (b) or (c).

However, regardless of the basis adopted, purchase price or production cost is to be determined in the same way as for all assets. These rules are set out in Chapter 4.

1981 1 sch 26

67 In describing the basis of valuation of stocks, 'market value' is only an appropriate phrase where a genuine market, e.g. The London Metal Exchange, exists. Where no such market exists, the term 'net realisable value' should be used.

68 Where a significant proportion of stocks held is subject to suppliers' reservation of title, it may be appropriate to disclose the facts and amounts involved.

69 In relation to the amount at which long term contracts are included there should be stated:

SSAP 9:27, 30

    (a) the amount of work in progress at cost plus attributable profit, less foreseeable losses;

    (b) cash received and receivable at the accounting date as payments on account of contracts in progress.

If losses recognised on individual contracts exceed costs incurred to date less progress payments received and receivable, such excesses should be shown separately as provisions at item C 9.

70   Items included as 'raw materials and consumables' which are constantly being replaced may be included at a fixed quantity and value, provided that: 1981 1 sch 25

    (a) their overall value is not material; and

    (b) their quantity, value and composition are not subject to material variation.

71   If there is a material difference between the value of stocks as included in the accounts and the value of stocks at replacement cost or most recent purchase or production cost (whichever the directors consider the more appropriate comparison), the amount of the difference must be stated in a note to the accounts.   1981 1 sch 27(3)–(5)

Debtors (item C II)
General

72   The amount falling due after more than one year must be shown separately for each item included under debtors.   1981 1 sch format note 5

73   Prepayments and accrued income may be shown in either of the two positions (item C II 6 or D) indicated in the standard formats.   1981 1 sch format note 6

Loans to and other transactions with directors

74   The provisions of the Companies Act 1980 in this area are complex. It is recommended that reference should be made to the Act itself and, in cases of doubt, legal advice should be sought. In general a company is, with certain specific exemptions, prohibited from making loans to or providing security for loans to directors. Nevertheless, details of any such transactions together with details of substantial contracts with directors must be disclosed, but corresponding figures for the previous year are not required. Where the company fails to make adequate disclosure the auditors must include the relevant information in their report.

Author

1980 s 54

1981 1 sch 58(3)
1980 s 59

75 Subject to certain specific exemptions below, the requirements to disclose apply to all transactions or arrangements whether or not: 1980 s 54(7)

  (a) they were unlawful; 1980 s 49–50

  (b) the director with whom they were made was a director or connected person at the time the transactions were made;

  (c) a company was a subsidiary of a company other than its current holding company when the transactions were made.

76 The transactions or arrangements concerned include principally: 1980 s 56(1)

  (a) loans;
  (b) guarantees;
  (c) provision of security;
  (d) quasi-loans;
  (e) credit transactions;
  (f) any other transaction or arrangement with a person who was a director at any time during the period, and who had, either directly or indirectly, a material interest in that transaction. 'Material' is not defined in the legislation, but it appears to apply primarily to the extent of the director's interest rather than to the size of the contract. 1980 s 54(1)(c), (2)(c), (3)

  Author

77 The transactions or arrangements to be disclosed include those between the company, or its subsidiary, and a director, or connected person, of the company or of its holding company. 1980 s 54(1)

78 Transactions and arrangements are deemed to include an agreement to make any such transaction or arrangement. 1980 s 54(1)(b)

79 A 'director' should be taken to include a 'shadow director', defined as a person in accordance with whose instructions the directors are accustomed to act, unless such instruction represents merely advice given in a professional capacity. 1980 s 63(1)

80 A 'connected person' is a spouse, child under 18 years of age, body corporate with which the director is associated, a trustee of a trust of which a director is a beneficiary, or a partner of the director or of any person connected with the director. 1980 s 64(1)–(2)

81 A 'quasi-loan' is defined as a transaction under which one party (the 'creditor') defrays or agrees to defray the expenditure of another (the 'borrower') either: 1980 s 65(2)

  (a) on terms that the borrower will reimburse the creditor; or

(b) in circumstances where the borrower becomes liable to reimburse the creditor.

82 A 'credit transaction' is a transaction under which one party (the 'creditor'):

1980 s 65(3)

(a) supplies any goods or sells any land under a hire purchase agreement or conditional sale agreement; or

(b) leases or hires any land or goods in return for periodical payments; or

(c) otherwise disposes of land or supplies goods or services on the understanding that payment (whether in a lump sum or instalments or by way of periodical payments or otherwise) is to be deferred.

83 The following particulars must be given in the notes to the accounts (by all companies other than recognised banks or their holding companies) for any transaction, arrangement or agreement required to be disclosed in respect of items referred to above:

1980 s 54(5), 55(1)

(a) A statement that it was made or subsisted during the year.

1980 s 55(1)(a)

(b) Names of directors (and, where relevant, connected persons) concerned and, for transactions to which section 54(1)(c) or section 54(2)(c) of the Companies Act 1980 applies (see above), the nature of the directors' interests.

1980 s 55(1)(b)—(c)

(c) Principal terms (including those relating to repayment, interest and security).

1980 s 55(1)
Author

(d) For loans, or agreements for or arrangements relating to loans:
(i) The amount of the liability (principal and interest) at the beginning and end of the year.
(ii) The maximum amount of the liability during the year.
(iii) The amount of any arrears of interest.
(iv) Any provision against non-repayment of the whole or any part of the principal or interest.

1980 s 55(1)(d)

Although loans by a company (and its subsidiaries) totalling a maximum of £2,500 and made to one of its directors (or to a holding company director) are now legal, full disclosure must still be made.

1980 s 50(2A)
(introduced by 1981 s 111(1))

(e) For guarantees or the provision of security, or agreements or arrangements relating thereto:
(i) The amount for which the company (or its subsidiary) was liable at the beginning and end of the year.

1980 s 55(1)(e)

(ii)   The maximum amount for which the company (or its subsidiary) may become so liable.

(iii)   Any amount or liability incurred in fulfilling the guarantee or discharging the security.

(f)   For any other transactions, arrangements or agreements, the value of the transaction or arrangement. For a quasi-loan value is the maximum amount liable to be repaid, and for a credit transaction value is the arm's length value of the goods or services concerned.   1980 s 55(1)(f)
1980 s 65(4)

84   Paragraph 10(l) of the Listing Agreement (requiring disclosure of directors' interests in significant contracts) has now been superseded by the provisions set out above. These provisions apply to all companies.

85   The following are exempted from the disclosure requirements set out above:

(a)   Service contracts between a company and its directors or directors of its holding company.   1980 s 54(6)(b)

(b)   Transactions, arrangements or agreements between two companies where a director is interested only by virtue of being a director of both companies.   1980 s 54(6)(a)

(c)   Transactions, arrangements or agreements with a director which, in aggregate, did not exceed £5,000 and which are credit transactions or related to credit transactions.   1980 s 58(1)–(2)

(d)   Transactions or arrangements (of the types envisaged by sections 54(1)(c) and 54(2)(c) of the 1980 Act) in which the director had a material interest if the value of each such transaction did not at any time in the year exceed in the aggregate: 1980 s 58(3)
(introduced by 1981 3 sch 53)
   (i)   £1,000; or if greater than £1,000
   (ii)   the lower of £5,000 or 1 per cent of the company's net assets at the year end.

(e)   Transactions or arrangements, or agreements relating thereto, which were made before 22 December 1980 and did not subsist on or after that day.   1980 s 54(6)(d)

86   Group accounts are required to show the above information only for holding company directors.   1981 1 sch 63(c), 68

Transactions with officers other than directors

87   In respect of each of the following categories (which include related guarantees, securities, arrangements and agreements to enter into such transactions):   1980 s 56(1)–(2)

(a) loans;

(b) quasi-loans; and

(c) credit transactions;

made between the company (and, in the case of a holding company, its subsidiaries) and persons who were officers of the company at any time during the year, there must be shown: 1980 s 56(2)

    (i)   the aggregate amounts outstanding at the end of the year;

    (ii)   the numbers of officers with whom such transactions or agreements were made;

however:

    (iii) no corresponding amounts need be shown for the previous year; and   1981 1 sch 58(3)

    (iv) consolidated accounts need only include the information relating to holding company officers.   1981 1 sch 63(c)

Where the aggregate amount due to the company (or group) from an officer at the year end under all transactions of the types mentioned above is less than £2,500, the information relating to that officer is not required to be included in the totals disclosed.   1980 s 56(2A) (introduced by 1981 3 sch 5?

88   There is no precise legal definition of an 'officer', although it has been established that the term includes company secretaries and general managers. It appears that an officer is a person acting in a decision making capacity, rather than one who merely implements the decisions of others. All persons named in the accounts as officers should be regarded as officers for the purpose of these disclosures.   1948 s 455 Author

89   There are special rules, outside the scope of this book, dealing with arrangements by recognised banks for their officers or their holding companies' officers.   1980 s 56(3)

Financial assistance for acquisition of shares

90   In cases where a company is permitted to give financial assistance for the acquisition of its own shares or shares in its holding company (see Chapter 12), there must be stated the aggregate amount of loans made in each of the following cases: 1981 1 sch 51(2) 1981 s 42(6)

(a) Loans made in accordance with an employees' share scheme.   1981 s 42(6)(b)

(b) Loans made to employees, other than directors, to enable those persons to acquire fully paid shares in the company or its holding company.   1981 s 42(6)(c)

(c) Permissible loans made by private companies.   1981 s 43

Called up share capital not paid (item A or C II 5)

91   Called up share capital not paid may be shown in either of the two positions indicated in the standard balance sheet formats.

1981 1 sch format note 1

Expenditure not to be Deferred

92   The following items of expenditure must not be treated as assets in any company's balance sheet and accordingly must be written off in the year in which they are incurred:

1981 1 sch 3(2)

(a)   Preliminary expenses.

(b)   Expenses of and commission on any issue of shares or debentures.

(c)   Costs of research.

The disclosure requirements for development expenditure carried forward are set out under 'Intangible fixed assets' above.

Called Up Share Capital (Item A I)

93   The amount of allotted share capital and the amount of called up share capital which has been paid up must each be shown separately.

1981 1 sch format note 12

94   The authorised share capital and, where shares of more than one class have been allotted, the number and aggregate nominal value of shares of each class allotted must be shown.

1981 1 sch 38(1)

Options on unissued shares

95   Where any option to subscribe or any other right (including conversion rights) to require the allotment of shares exists, the number, description and amount of shares, together with the option price and period in which it is exercisable must be shown.

1981 1 sch 40

Shares held beneficially by subsidiary companies

96   The number, description and amount of any shares of the company held beneficially by its subsidiary companies or their nominees must be shown in a note to the accounts.

1981 1 sch 60

Preference shares

97   Where the title of a class of preference shares (or participating preference or preferred ordinary shares) issued before 6 April 1973 includes a fixed rate of dividend, the rate of dividend appropriate after that date i.e. adjusted to take account of the imputation basis of taxation, should be incorporated in the description of the shares in the balance sheet.

SSAP 8:28

Redeemable shares

98   Where redeemable shares have been issued, there must be disclosed: 1981 1 sch 38(2)

    (a)   the earliest and latest dates of redemption;
    (b)   whether redemption is mandatory or at the option of the company;
    (c)   the premium, if any, payable on redemption.

Arrears of dividend

99   The amount of arrears of fixed cumulative dividend (excluding related ACT)   1981 1 sch 49
for each class of shares and the period over which the arrears have
accumulated must be disclosed.

Allotment of shares

100   For each class of share allotted during the year there must be shown the   1981 1 sch 39
number of shares, aggregate nominal value, consideration received and
reason for making the allotment.

Reserves (Items A II, III, IV, V)

101   Reserves should not include any amount which falls within the definition of a
provision as set out below. Reserves are not defined in law (except in the case
of companies covered by schedule 8A to the Companies Act 1948), but may
be taken to be that part of shareholders' funds not accounted for by the
nominal value of issued share capital or by the share premium account.

102   The notes to the accounts should give details of reserves which the company
does not regard as distributable where this is not apparent from the account
heading.

103   Reserves not set aside for a specific purpose should normally be combined,
insofar as they are properly regarded as distributable, with the balance on
the profit and loss account and included as item A V.

104   Any other non-distributable reserves not specifically mentioned in the
formats (e.g. reserves arising on consolidation) might fall to be included
under item A IV 4.

105   All movements on those reserves listed in either of the standard formats must   1981 1 sch 46
be shown, giving a reconciliation between the opening and closing balances
with explanations of transfers to or from the reserve. Corresponding figures
for the previous year are not required for this reconciliation.   1981 1 sch 58(3)

106   Material prior year adjustments should be accounted for by restating prior   SSAP 6:16
years' figures. With that exception, additions to and withdrawals from

retained profit and the application of other reserves to the relief of charges on revenue should be passed through the profit and loss account.

107 The balance on the profit and loss account must be shown in the position laid down by the formats, even in the case of a debit balance.

108 If government grants are not deducted from the cost of the related assets, the deferred credit, if material, should be disclosed as deferred income at item D in the balance sheet format, not as a reserve.

SSAP 4:9

Investment revaluation reserve

109 Changes in the value of investment properties should not be reflected in the profit and loss account, but should be transferred to an investment revaluation reserve. The reserve should be prominently displayed in the balance sheet. It will normally be appropriate to include the investment revaluation reserve within item A III and make separate disclosure in the notes. Any deficit arising on the investment revaluation reserve should be charged in the profit and loss account.

SSAP 19:13, 15

Author

Provisions for Liabilities and Charges (Item B)

Definition

110 A provision for liabilities and charges is defined as an amount retained as reasonably necessary for the purpose of providing for any liability or loss which is either likely to be incurred, or certain to be incurred but uncertain as to amount or as to the date on which it will arise.

1981 1 sch 88

Movements on provision accounts

111 Where any amount is transferred to any of those provisions for liabilities or charges listed in either of the standard formats, or is transferred from any such provision otherwise than for the purpose for which it was created, a reconciliation must be given between the opening and closing balances on the provision with explanations of transfers to or from the provision. Corresponding figures for the previous year are not required for this reconciliation.

1981 1 sch 46

1981 1 sch 58(3)

Taxation provisions

112 Deferred taxation must be included in the formats under item B 2, and taxation payable under item C 8. However B 2 must also include any taxation provisions which are neither deferred taxation nor taxation payable, for example a provision for items disputed with the Inland Revenue, and the amount provided must be stated.

Author

1981 1 sch 47

113 Where amounts of deferred taxation arise which relate to movements on reserves (e.g. resulting from a revaluation of assets) the amounts transferred

SSAP 15:38

to or from deferred taxation account should be shown separately as part of such movements.

114   Where the value of an asset is shown by way of a note on the face of or annexed to the accounts and that value differs from the book value of the asset, the note should also show, if material, the tax implications which would result from the realisation of the asset at the balance sheet date at the stated value.   SSAP 15:39

115   Where only part of the full potential deferred tax liability is provided, the nature and the amount of the major elements of which that balance is comprised should be stated, together with a description of the method of calculation adopted. The amount of deferred tax not provided should be based on substantiated calculations and assumptions which are explained in the accounts.   SSAP 15:30, 37

116   The extent of the explanation referred to above is not specified in SSAP 15. The accounts should, however, contain sufficient information to indicate to the reader what assumptions have been used by management without going so far as to prejudice commercial confidentiality or to provide a quantified forecast.

117   Similar explanations to those required in respect of partial provisions are also desirable if none of the potential liability has been provided.

118   The full potential amount of the deferred tax liability should be disclosed by way of note, distinguishing between the various principal categories of deferred taxation and showing for each category the amount that has been provided in the accounts.   SSAP 15:33

Creditors (Item C)

General

119   Where balance sheet format 2 is adopted, each item included under creditors (liabilities, item C) must be split between the amounts payable within one year and after one year, and separate totals are to be shown. Format 1 provides for this analysis to be given on the face of the balance sheet.   1981 1 sch format note 13

120   For each item shown under creditors (whichever balance sheet format is adopted) there must be stated the aggregate amount of any debts which: 1981 1 sch 48(1)

    (a)   are payable otherwise than by instalments and fall due for payment after the end of the five year period following the end of the financial year; or

(b)   are payable by instalments any of which fall due for payment after that period;

and, in the case of (b), the amount falling due after the five year period must also be shown.

121   Terms of repayment and interest rates for every item included under 'creditors' must be shown.   1981 1 sch 48(2)

122   If such a statement would be, in the view of the directors, excessively long, a general indication of repayment terms and interest rates will be sufficient.   1981 1 sch 48(3)

123   For each item under creditors for which security has been given, an indication of the nature of the security given and the aggregate amount of debts included under that item covered by the security must be stated. In giving 'an indication of the nature of the security', it will probably be acceptable to describe the charge in general terms, referring, for example, to 'mortgages on freehold land and buildings' rather than specifying the particular properties involved.   1981 1 sch 48(4)

Author

124   In addition, listed companies are required to state in respect of bank loans and overdrafts and other borrowings of the company, the aggregate amounts repayable: LA para 10(f)

(a)   in one year or less, or on demand;
(b)   between one and two years;
(c)   between two and five years; and
(d)   in five years or more.

Borrowing powers

125   If limits are imposed upon the company's borrowing powers by its articles or debenture trust deeds, and those limits are exceeded at the year end, the facts and amounts involved together with a statement as to what is being done to rectify the situation should be disclosed in a note to the accounts.

Debentures (item C 1)

126   There is no precise definition of a debenture, either in law or practice. It is essentially a formal acknowledgement of a debt, although the term is often applied to the debt itself.

127   Debentures are usually, but need not be, secured; and there may or may not be a trust deed to set out the respective rights of the company and the debenture holders.

128   If the company has issued any debentures during the financial year there must be stated: 1981 1 sch 41(1)

       (a)   the reason for making the issue;

       (b)   the classes of debentures issued; and

       (c)   for each class, the amount issued and the consideration received for the issue.

129   The number, description and amount of any debenture of the company held beneficially by its subsidiaries, or their nominees, must be shown in a note to the accounts.   1981 1 sch 60

130   The amount of any convertible loans must be shown separately.   1981 1 sch format note 7

Redeemed debentures

131   Particulars must be given of redeemed debentures which the company has the power to reissue. Redeemed debentures may be reissued unless: 1981 1 sch 41(2)   1948 s 90(1)

       (a)   a provision to the contrary is contained in the articles, or in a contract; or

       (b)   the company has passed a resolution to the effect that they shall be cancelled.

Dividends

132   The provision for the recommended dividend must be separately stated. Since the standard formats do not contain a separate heading for dividends payable, the recommended dividend will normally be included as a current liability, under item C8, but disclosed in the notes to the accounts. It is not necessary to state separately the amount of any dividends already declared but unpaid at the balance sheet date.   1981 1 sch 51(3)

    Author

133   ACT on recommended dividends should not be included in the figures given in the above paragraph, but should be included as a current tax liability.   SSAP 8:26

Tax liabilities

134   Liabilities, as opposed to provisions, for taxation must be included in the balance sheet under C8 'other creditors including taxation and social security', with the liability for taxation and social security being shown separately from 'other creditors'. Depending on the date to which a company makes up its accounts, the balance sheet should contain either: 1981 1 sch format note 9

    SSAP 8:14

(a) one liability for mainstream corporation tax, being that on the profit of the year; or

(b) two liabilities.

In the latter case the liabilities will be respectively for:

  (i)   the mainstream corporation tax on the profits of the previous year payable within nine months of the balance sheet date; and

  (ii) mainstream corporation tax for the year under review payable 12 months later than the above liability. These liabilities must be separately disclosed, as a consequence of the requirement to analyse creditors between amounts due within one year and after one year.

1981 1 sch format note 13

135   ACT on dividends paid before the year end, if it is regarded as recoverable, should be deducted from the full corporation tax charge on the profit of the year in arriving at the mainstream corporation tax liability shown in the balance sheet.

SSAP 8:15

136   If the ACT on proposed dividends is regarded as recoverable, it should be deducted from the deferred tax account, if such an account is available for this purpose. In the absence of a deferred taxation account if the ACT is regarded as recoverable it may, under the new rules, be put into the balance sheet formats as a prepayment, with disclosure if realisation is more than one year hence.

SSAP 8:27

Author

137   Realisation may be less than one year from the balance sheet date where substantial amounts of franked investment income are regularly received, for example by an investment trust company.

138   The ACT on proposed dividends (whether recoverable or irrecoverable) should be included under creditors (item C 8) as a current taxation liability. The tax credit in respect of surplus franked investment income should be deducted from the current liability for ACT.

SSAP 8:26

139   The net amount due to (or from) the Customs and Excise in respect of VAT should be included as part of creditors (or debtors) and will not normally require separate disclosure.

SSAP 5:5

Payments received on account (item C 3)

140   Payments received on account, insofar as they are not shown as deductions from stocks, must be disclosed separately. This will normally only give rise to a creditor where the payments are in excess of the amount at which the relevant work in progress is stated.

1981 1 sch format note 8
Author

Accruals and deferred income (item C 9 or D)

141 Accruals and deferred income must be shown either as a separate heading in the balance sheet or as a ·subheading of creditors. If there are significant amounts of non-current deferred income (e.g. the deferred credit in respect of regional development grants), it may be appropriate to segregate such amounts and show them under item H 9, rather than E 9, where balance sheet format 1 is adopted.

1981 1 sch format note 10
Author

142 The liability for items such as goods or services received but uninvoiced at the balance sheet date should be treated as a trade creditor (item C 4), rather than an accrual (items C 9 or D).

Net Current Assets/Liabilities

143 Where format 1 is adopted any amounts shown under 'prepayments and accrued income' must be taken into account when calculating net current assets, whether such prepayments are shown as format item C II 6 or D.

1981 1 sch format note 11

Pension Funds, Unfunded Pensions, Indemnities and Compensation to Staff

144 Details must be given of any pension commitments provided for in the company's balance sheet, and also of any such commitments for which no provision has been made. Particulars of pension commitments to past directors of the company must be disclosed separately.

1981 1 sch 50(4)

145 A brief description of the company's pension arrangements is recommended, which should include the following minimum disclosure:

(a) The extent to which the employees are covered.
(b) Whether or not the fund is contributory.
(c) The amount of any estimated underfunding.
(d) If (c) above is applicable, the manner in which the deficiency is to be made good.

Guarantees and Other Financial Commitments

146 Particulars of charges on assets to secure the liabilities of any other person with, where practicable, the amount secured must be stated.

1981 1 sch 50(1)

147 The following information must be given in respect of any contingent liability (other than those above) insofar as it has not been provided and the possibility of loss is not remote:

1981 1 sch 50(2)
SSAP 18:16, 18–19

(a) The estimated amount of the liability not provided in the accounts.
(b) Its legal nature.
(c) Whether any security has been given and, if so, what.

In addition there should be stated: SSAP 18:18

(d) the factors affecting the likelihood of the liability crystallising; and
(e) if an estimate of the financial effect cannot be made, a statement to that effect.

148 The estimated financial effect of contingencies should be disclosed before   SSAP 18:20
taxation, the taxation implications if the contingencies crystallise being
explained separately.

149 Contingent gains should not be accrued, and should only be disclosed if the   SSAP 18:17
realisation of the gain is probable. If disclosure is made the information set
out above should be given (with the exception of details regarding security).

150 The aggregate amount of contracted capital expenditure not provided, and   1981 1 sch 50(3)
the amount authorised by directors but not contracted, must be shown where
practicable. Capital commitments should include the amount of any   SSAP 5:6, 9
irrecoverable VAT.

151 Details of any other financial commitments which have not been provided   1981 1 sch 50(5)
and which are relevant to assessing the company's state of affairs must be
shown. This provision is very widely drawn, and might include, for example,   Author
unmatched forward foreign exchange contracts.

152 Financial commitments are unlikely to include the company's normal sales
and purchase order books, its liability to continue to pay wages, or matched
foreign exchange commitments.

153 The disclosure above in respect of guarantees, commitments and pension   1981 1 sch 50(6)
funds must include separately details of commitments on behalf of, or for the
benefit of:

(a) any holding company or fellow subsidiary of the company; and
(b) any subsidiary of the company.

154 An example of a circumstance which might involve disclosure under the
above paragraph is the existence of cross-guarantees under a group banking
scheme.

155 SSAP 17 requires non-adjusting events, and the reversal of window-dressing
transactions, to be disclosed in the accounts. There is a conflict between this
requirement and the Companies Act 1981, which requires disclosure of
important post balance sheet events in the directors' report. The
requirements are explained, the conflict analysed and a mode of disclosure
suggested, in Chapter 2.

156   If non-adjusting post balance sheet events are disclosed in the directors'
        report instead of in the accounts, cross-reference in the accounts to the
        relevant paragraph in the directors' report might be thought to be helpful but
        in the author's view would not be regarded as mandatory.

Identity of Ultimate Holding Company

157   Every subsidiary company must disclose in a note to its accounts the name   1967 s 5
        and, if known, the country of incorporation of the company regarded by the
        directors as its ultimate holding company at the end of the financial year. If
        the subsidiary carries on business outside the United Kingdom and
        disclosure of the name of the ultimate holding company would in the opinion
        of the directors be harmful to the subsidiary, the ultimate holding company,
        or any fellow subsidiary, then with the consent of the Department of Trade
        such disclosure need not be made.

Date of Approval of Accounts by Directors

158   The date on which the accounts were approved by the board of directors   SSAP 17:26
        should be disclosed in the accounts.

6 Profit and Loss Account

Definition

1   The term profit and loss account includes, in the case of a company not trading for profit, an income and expenditure account.

1948 s 149(8)(b) (introduced by 1981 s 1(1))

Groups

2   Groups preparing consolidated accounts are not required to include the parent company profit and loss account in their annual accounts, and few do so. The requirements set out in this chapter apply in the case of groups to the consolidated profit and loss account, except for certain items, identified in Chapter 8, which apply to the parent company even if a consolidated profit and loss account is presented.

Format

3   Four alternative formats are permitted for the profit and loss account, and the rules governing their modification are set out in Chapter 3 of this book. All the items listed in the standard profit and loss account formats are assigned Arabic numerals and accordingly may under certain circumstances be combined together on the face of the profit and loss account. In the interest of clear presentation, it is undesirable for immaterial items to be shown. Advantage may also be taken of the format rules for combination of material items, which should then be disclosed in the notes to the accounts.

1981 1 sch 1

1981 1 sch 3(4)

4   A statement of retained profits showing any prior year adjustment should immediately follow the profit and loss account for the year.

SSAP 6:17

Modified Accounts

5   Companies preparing 'modified accounts' should refer to Chapter 10, which explains how the rules set out in this chapter are to be modified in their circumstances.

51

General

6   In addition to the items required by the standard formats, every profit and loss account must show:

    (a)   profit or loss on ordinary activities before taxation;   1981 1 sch 3(6)

    (b)   any amount transferred or proposed to be transferred to or from   1981 1 sch 3(7)(a)
         reserves;

    (c)   the aggregate amount of dividends paid or proposed excluding both the   1981 1 sch 3(7)(b)
         related ACT or attributable tax credit.   SSAP 8:24

7   If either format 1 or format 3 is adopted, 'cost of sales', 'distribution costs'   1981 1 sch format
    and 'administrative expenses' must be stated after taking account of   note 14
    provisions for depreciation or diminution in value of assets.

8   The profit and loss account must disclose: 1981 1 sch format
                                                      SSAP 6:17

    (a)   profit or loss after taxation but before extraordinary items;

    (b)   the amount of any extraordinary items, and the attributable taxation;

    (c)   profit or loss after extraordinary items, reflecting all profits and losses   SSAP 6:13
         recognised in the accounts of the year other than material prior year
         adjustments and unrealised surpluses on revaluation of fixed assets.

    There must also be stated, either on the face of the profit and loss account, or   1981 1 sch 57(2)
    by note, particulars of the extraordinary items. As a result, the 1981 Act has   SSAP 6:15
    effectively embodied SSAP 6:13, 15 and 17. Extraordinary items are not   Author
    defined in the 1981 Act, but are defined in SSAP 6 as those items which derive   SSAP 6:11
    from events or transactions outside the ordinary activities of the business and
    which are both material and not expected to recur frequently or regularly.

Exceptional Items

9   Items regarded as exceptional due to their abnormal size or incidence but   1981 1 sch 57(3)
    which are derived from the ordinary activities of the business must be   SSAP 6:5, 14
    included in arriving at the profit or loss before taxation and extraordinary
    items. The nature and amount of such items must be disclosed.

Profit or Loss on Disposal of Fixed Assets

10   The amount of any material profit or loss arising from the disposal of fixed   SSAP 12:6
    assets should be separately disclosed.

Adjustments Relating to Prior Years

11 Material adjustments (less attributable taxation) applicable to prior years arising from changes in accounting policies and from the correction of fundamental errors should be accounted for by restating prior years, with the result that the opening balance of retained profit will be adjusted. The effect of the change or correction must be disclosed.

SSAP 6:16

1981 1 sch 4(2)

12 Where any material amount relating to any preceding financial year is included in any item in the profit and loss account, the effect must be stated. Items representing the normal recurring correction and adjustment of accounting estimates made in prior years should be included in the result for the year before tax and extraordinary items, and need be disclosed as to size and nature only if material.

1981 1 sch 57(1), 85

SSAP 6:16

Information Supplementing the Profit and Loss Account

13 The further information set out below is required to supplement the profit and loss account and must, unless stated otherwise, be given either in the profit and loss account or in the notes.

1981 1 sch 35

Analysis of turnover and profit

14 Turnover is defined as the amounts derived from the provision of goods and services falling within the company's ordinary activities, after deduction of trade discounts, value added tax and any other taxes based on the amounts so derived.

1981 1 sch 94

SSAP 5:8

15 For each class of business which in the opinion of the directors is substantially different from other businesses carried on there must be disclosed:

1981 1 sch 55(1)

(a) the amount of turnover attributable to that class; and

(b) the profit or loss before taxation attributable, in the opinion of the directors, to that class.

16 In deciding what constitutes a different class of business or market, the directors must consider the manner in which the company's activities are organised. This can be taken to give the directors considerable powers of discretion in interpreting 'substantially different'. It will normally be sufficient to limit the analysis to those activities which, in the opinion of the directors, are clearly distinct from one another. Different stages in a manufacturing and distribution process (i.e. vertical integration) might not be regarded as different businesses for this purposes, since the allocation of

1981 1 sch 55(3)

Author

profits between such different stages is likely to be arbitrary and therefore not meaningful.

17   For each geographical market which, in the opinion of the directors, is substantially different, the turnover attributable to that market must be shown.   1981 1 sch 55(2)

18   The Listing Agreement requires information broadly similar to the above, and in addition a geographical analysis of turnover and trading profit derived from operations outside the United Kingdom and Eire should be given, where such turnover exceeds 10 per cent of total turnover. The disclosures required are: LA para 10(c)

  (a)   an analysis of turnover by continent and, if any continent accounts for more than 50 per cent of turnover derived from such overseas operations, a more detailed breakdown (e.g. by country); and

  (b)   an analysis of trading results if the contribution from a specific area is abnormal.

19   Classes of business or markets which, in the opinion of the directors, do not differ substantially are to be treated as one class or market, and any immaterial amounts attributable to one class of business or market must be included in the amount stated in respect of another class or market.   1981 1 sch 55(4)

20   Difficulties may be experienced in the fair allocation of head office or similar expenses to different business classes. In such circumstances it may be preferable to show the gross contributions to profit of each class of business, with a deduction from the total of such gross contributions in respect of the unallocated charges.

21   Where, in the opinion of the directors, disclosure of the above information on turnover and profit would be seriously prejudicial to the interests of the company, the information need not be disclosed provided the accounts include a statement to that effect.   1981 1 sch 55(5)

22   In the accounts of a subsidiary company, it may be appropriate to indicate the extent of sales to other group companies (if material), in order to assist the presentation of a true and fair view.

Income from rents

23   Income from rents from land and buildings (after deduction of ground rents, rates and other outgoings), must be disclosed if such rents form a substantial part of the company's revenue.   1981 1 sch 53(5)

Income from investments

24   Income from listed investments, including any tax credit in respect of incoming dividends from UK resident companies, must be disclosed.   1981 1 sch 53(4)
SSAP 8:25

25   Income derived from fixed asset investments must be split between that derived from group companies and that derived from other sources.   1981 1 sch format note 15

Other income

26   Other income must be distinguished between that due from group companies and that derived from other sources.   1981 1 sch format note 15

27   Where material revenue based government grants have been credited to the profit and loss account, this fact, and the amount involved, should be disclosed.

Auditors' remuneration

28   The auditors' remuneration, including expenses, must be shown. Fees for other work need not be disclosed.   1981 1 sch 53(7)
Author

Emoluments, pensions and compensation paid to directors and past directors

29   The amounts described in the three categories set out below must be disclosed in a note to the accounts, irrespective of materiality, distinguishing in each case between amounts receivable as directors (e.g. fees, percentages and remuneration for special services) and other amounts receivable (e.g. in respect of management or executive positions) for services to the company or to its subsidiary companies. Directors are to apportion payments, where necessary, to analyse them into the above categories. The payments to be disclosed are as follows: 1948 s 196(2)–(4)

       1948 s 196(7)

   (a)   Aggregate of directors' emoluments including fees, percentages, expense allowances charged to United Kingdom income tax, pension scheme contributions and estimated money value of any other benefits received otherwise than in cash.   1948 s 196(1)(a), (2)

   (b)   Aggregate of pensions payable to directors or their nominees or dependants (excluding pensions payable under a pension scheme where the contributions are substantially adequate for the maintenance of the scheme).   1948 s 196(1)(b), (3)

   (c)   Aggregate of compensation in respect of loss of office, including retirement, paid to past directors. (The payment to a director of such compensation is illegal unless particulars and the amount of the proposed payment have been disclosed to and approved by the company in general meeting. Compensation for loss of office does not   1948 s 196(1)(c), (4)
1948 s 191–194

       1948 s 194(2)–(3)

include any bona fide payment representing damages for breach of contract or consideration for the premature termination of a service agreement, or a pension, any of which would be included under either (a) or (b) above.)

30   Particulars must include sums paid by or receivable from: 1948 s 196(5)(a)

(a)   the company;

(b)   the company's subsidiaries;

(c)   any other person, but not sums for which the recipient has to account.

In regard to compensation for loss of office, there must be shown separately the amounts received from each of the above sources.   1948 s 196(5)(b)

31   Where the recipient has not accounted for monies received within two years, or where an expense allowance has been charged to United Kingdom income tax at a later date, the relevant sums must be included in the next succeeding accounts, and shown separately.   1948 s 196(6)

32   There is a special definition of a subsidiary for the purpose of section 196. When any director of the company is or was by virtue of the company's direct or indirect nomination at the same time a director of any other body corporate, that body must for this purpose be treated as a subsidiary company.   1948 s 196(9)

33   In respect of the emoluments of the directors (excluding for this purpose contributions paid by the company under any pension scheme) there must be stated: 1967 s 6(3)

(a)   the number of directors whose emoluments fall into each bracket of a scale in multiples of £5,000. Individual brackets need only be shown where the emoluments of at least one of the directors fall within the bracket in either the current or previous year. Directors who have no emoluments should be included in the bracket from £nil to £5,000;   1967 s 6(1)(b) SI 1979 No 1618

(b)   the emoluments while chairman of each person so acting during the year;   1967 s 6(1)(a)

(c)   the emoluments of highest paid director if not the chairman. It is not necessary to give the name of such director.   1967 s 6(2), (7) Author

Items (a), (b) and (c) are not applicable to a director whose duties were carried   1967 s 6(1)(a)–(b), (2)

out wholly or mainly outside the United Kingdom, or to a company which is neither a holding company nor a subsidiary company and the aggregate directors' emoluments of which (excluding for this purpose pensions and any compensation for loss of office) do not exceed £40,000.

1967 s 6(6)
SI 1979 No 1618

34   The number of directors who have waived rights to receive emoluments, including pension contributions, during the year and the aggregate amount thereof must be shown. This is not applicable to a company which is neither a holding company nor a subsidiary company and the aggregate directors' emoluments of which (excluding for this purpose pensions and compensation for loss of office) do not exceed £40,000. Listed companies are to give details of waivers of future emoluments by directors, whether receivable from the company or its subsidiaries.

1967 s 7(1), (3)
SI 1979 No 1618

LA para 10(m)

35   A consolidated profit and loss account need only disclose the details relating to the holding company directors.

1981 1 sch 63(a)

Number of employees receiving more than £20,000 per annum

36   In respect of employees receiving more than £20,000 per annum (excluding contributions paid under any pension scheme), the number of employees other than directors whose emoluments fall in each bracket of a scale in multiples of £5,000, starting at £20,000, must be shown. Individual brackets need only be shown where the emoluments of at least one employee fall within that bracket in either the current or the previous year. Employees whose duties were performed wholly or mainly outside the United Kingdom may be left out of account for this purpose.

1967 s 8
SI 1979 No 1618

37   Disclosure in group accounts need only relate to those executives who are in the employment of the holding company, and for this purpose emoluments received from all group companies should be aggregated.

1981 1 sch 63(b)

38   The auditors must give in their report the details of directors' and higher paid employees' emoluments should the company fail to do so.

1948 s 196(8)
1967 s 6(4), 7(3), 8(4)

Staff

39   There must be stated:

(a)   the average number of persons employed in the financial year (whether in the United Kingdom or abroad);

1981 1 sch 56(1)(a)

(b)   the average number of such employees within each category of persons employed. Categories must be determined by the directors having regard to the manner in which the company's activities are organised. It is not clear what sort of categories are envisaged. The options appear to be:

1981 1 sch 56(1)(b), (5)

Author

(i)   a geographical analysis;

(ii)   a functional analysis (production, marketing, administration, etc);
      or

(iii)   an analysis by product group.

The 'average number' must be calculated by dividing the total of the numbers of staff employed under contracts of service in each week of the financial year by the number of weeks in the financial year.   1981 1 sch 56(2)–(3)

40   It seems clear that the above information must be given in respect of all employees, both in the United Kingdom and abroad. The disclosure in respect of emoluments and the average number of employees should make it clear whether or not executive directors have been included.

41   In respect of the same persons taken into account in the preceding paragraph, there must be stated separately the aggregate amounts of: 1981 1 sch 56(4)

(a)   wages and salaries paid or payable for the year in respect of those persons;

(b)   social security costs incurred by the company on their behalf;

(c)   other pension costs so incurred, insofar as any of these amounts are included in the profit and loss account.

Depreciation

42   Any charges for depreciation and diminution in value of fixed assets must be stated by note, if not otherwise required to be shown by the profit and loss account format adopted. In addition there must be stated separately the aggregate amounts of: 1981 1 sch format note 17

(a)   any provision against a fixed asset investment for diminution in value;   1981 1 sch 19(1)

(b)   any provision against a fixed asset for permanent diminution in value;   1981 1 sch 19(2)

(c)   any write back of a provision made under (a) or (b) above which is no longer necessary.   1981 1 sch 19(3)

Related companies

43   Related companies are defined in Chapter 5, where it was suggested that there is likely to be little practical difference between the concepts of related and associated companies. For consistency, reference is made to related companies, although strictly SSAP 1 only applies to associates.

44   SSAP 1 contains the following requirements regarding the accounting treatment and disclosure in respect of the results of related companies in the consolidated profit and loss account:

(a)   There should be included in the investing group's consolidated profit   SSAP 1:10, 14–17
and loss account the investing group's share of profits less losses of all material related companies. In particular, there should be separate disclosure of the investing group's share of related companies':
(i)   profits less losses before taxation;
(ii)   taxation (within group tax charge);
(iii)   extraordinary items (to be aggregated with the investing group's extraordinary items if not material to the investing group);
(iv)   profits less losses retained.

(b)   The group's share of related companies' turnover and depreciation   SSAP 1:18
should not be aggregated in consolidated accounts.

(c)   If the results of one or more related companies are of such significance in   SSAP 1:18
the context of the investing group's accounts that more detailed information about these would assist in giving a true and fair view, this information should be given by separate disclosure of the total turnover of the related companies concerned, their total depreciation charge, their total profits less losses before taxation and the amounts of such profits attributable to the investing group.

45   This is supported by the 1981 Act effectively providing that the results of   1981 1 sch 65(1)
related companies may be equity accounted in the consolidated profit and loss account. The Act does not use the term related companies in this context but instead refers to companies which are 'so closely associated with a member of the group' as to justify the equity method. In practice this requirement will normally only be met by associated companies as defined by SSAP 1 or certain subsidiaries excluded from consolidation.

46   SSAP 1 requires that the investor's own profit and loss account should   Author
include:

(a)   dividends received up to the accounting date of the investing company;   SSAP 1:7(a)(i)
and

(b)   dividends receivable in respect of accounting years ending on or before   SSAP 1:7(a)(ii)
that date and declared before the accounts of the investing company are approved by its directors.

In normal circumstances this is consistent with the 1981 Act, which makes no   Author
reference to the inclusion of related companies' results in the investor's own profit and loss account.

47   However, difficulties can arise if the investor has no subsidiaries and therefore does not prepare consolidated accounts. (This problem does not arise in relation to intermediate holding companies that do not prepare consolidated accounts, because the requirement of SSAP 1:8 — see below — is not normally regarded as applicable in these circumstances.)

48   SSAP 1 requires the profit and loss account to be 'adapted' to give the information regarding share of profits. The 1981 Act may be interpreted to preclude this by reason of the absence of reference to the equity method of accounting in this context, and by the requirement that only realised profits may be included in the profit and loss account. While recognising the doubt as to the legal position, the authors consider that the following treatment will not conflict with the law on the grounds that (i) by being recommended in an Accounting Standard, it forms part of generally accepted accounting principles, and (ii) it does not represent 'the equity method of accounting' in that the investor's share of retained profits is segregated into a revaluation reserve: *SSAP 1:8*

1981 1 sch 90
Author

     (a)   The investor's share of the related company's results is included and disclosed in the investor's profit and loss account exactly as in a consolidated profit and loss account.

     (b)   The investor's share of the related company's retained profits for the year is removed from the balance on the profit and loss account and transferred to the revaluation reserve.

49   The investor's share of accumulated retained profits would be:

     (a)   included in the carrying value of the investment in the balance sheet, if the investment is dealt with on the equity method of valuation; or

     (b)   disclosed by way of note, if the investment is carried at cost.

50   In order to accommodate equity accounting in the consolidated accounts, some adaptation of the standard profit and loss formats will be necessary, since initially the line in the standard formats 'Income from shares in related companies' could be interpreted only to include dividends receivable. It is therefore suggested that:

     (a) (i)   the line 'Income from shares in related companies' should be included in the notes to the accounts, with disclosure of the dividend income received from such companies, analysed between that attributable to listed and to unlisted investments; and

          (ii)   a new line be inserted into the profit and loss account entitled 'Share of profits less losses of related companies';

(b) the line 'Tax on profit or loss on ordinary activities' should be split either on the face of the profit and loss account or in the notes, between that applicable to:

    (i)   the investing company and its subsidiaries; and

    (ii)   the related companies.

Interest payable and similar charges

51   Interest payable (gross) or other similar charges must be disclosed showing separately the totals of interest payable on loans from group companies, and all other interest payable. In the latter case, the totals of interest on loans in each of the following categories must be shown separately:

1981 1 sch 53(2)
1981 1 sch format note 16

(a) All bank loans and overdrafts, together with other loans (other than from group companies) either:

    (i)   not repayable by instalments and due for repayment within five years of the year end; or

    (ii)   repayable by instalments the last of which falls due within five years of the year end.

(b) All other loans (other than from group companies).

Examples of 'other similar charges' might include the discount on bills of exchange and the interest element of hire purchase charges.

Author

Hire of plant and machinery

52   Amounts charged to revenue for hire of plant and machinery must be shown. Such amounts should include any charges paid under non-capitalised leases for plant and machinery.

1981 1 sch 53(6)

Author

53   The words 'plant and machinery' should be construed to cover whatever items in the nature of fixed assets (other than land and buildings) are hired for use in the business, e.g. vehicles, ships or other equipment.

Taxation

54   The charge for taxation must be shown, distinguishing between:

1981 1 sch 54
SSAP 8:22
SSAP 15:34

(a) United Kingdom corporation tax, showing the extent of any relief from double taxation;

(b) any material transfers between the deferred taxation account and the profit and loss account. The statutory provisions on deferred tax are extended by SSAP 15, which requires that deferred taxation dealt with in the profit and loss account should be shown separately as a component of the total tax charge or credit in the profit and loss account, or by way of note to the accounts;

(c) United Kingdom income tax (e.g. tax attributable to franked investment income);

(d) overseas taxation of profits, income and capital gains (so far as the tax is charged to revenue), relieved and unrelieved, specifying that part of the unrelieved overseas taxation which arises from the payment or proposed payment of dividends;

(e) irrecoverable ACT.

The amounts shown above must be stated separately in respect of 'tax on profit or loss on ordinary activities' and 'tax on extraordinary profit or loss'.

1981 1 sch 54(3)
SSAP 15:36

55   The basis on which United Kingdom corporation tax is computed must be stated; SSAP 8 requires the tax to be based on the profit of the year.

1981 1 sch 54(1)
SSAP 8:22(a)

56   If the rate of corporation tax is not known for the whole or part of the year, the latest known rate should be used and disclosed.

SSAP 8:23

57   Any material adjustment in respect of amounts charged in previous years should be shown separately but normally included in arriving at the tax charge or credit for the year.

SSAP 6:5

58   If material trading losses are set off against chargeable capital gains for corporation tax purposes, appropriate adjustments should be made in the accounts to make clear the true incidence of tax suffered and relieved.

59   Disclosure must be made of any special circumstances which affect the liability in respect of taxation of profits, income or capital gains for the year under review or succeeding years. These might include such items as:

1981 1 sch 54(2)

Author

(a) disallowable expenses;

(b) tax free income;

(c) losses, either revenue or capital and including previously unutilised allowances or stock appreciation relief, brought forward and utilised in the year;

(d) losses, as described in (c) above, incurred during the year but not utilised and therefore available for use in future years. The tax effect of such losses may be:
   (i) carried forward in the accounts by deduction from the deferred tax balance or (exceptionally) as an asset; or
   (ii) disclosed by way of note. Such note should make it clear that any tax relief is dependent on there being future profits (revenue or capital, as the case may be) of sufficient amount;

(e) losses set off against the profits of the preceding accounting period;

(f) the surrender or claim of losses by way of group relief, or the surrender or claim of ACT (to be disclosed in the accounts of the companies concerned) either:
   (i) paid for (or to be paid for) by the claiming company; or
   (ii) surrendered free of charge;

(g) the potential recovery in future years of presently irrecoverable ACT, or a potential tax credit on surplus franked investment income. The disclosure of the potential benefit should be such that it is clear that the benefit depends:
   (i) in the case of irrecoverable ACT, on there being future taxable profits of sufficient amount; and
   (ii) in the case of surplus franked investment income, on the company making future distributions;

(h) the realisation in the year of the benefits described in (g) brought forward from previous years;

(i) the deferral of tax on capital gains under 'rollover' provisions;

(j) the effect on potential tax liabilities arising from the apportionment of income of a close company.

Disclosure of such matters should be restricted to those where the tax effect is significant. The statutory provision above does not require the effect of the special circumstances of the tax charge to be quantified, but merely the circumstances identified. However, if more than one of the circumstances outlined in the preceding paragraph arises to a significant extent, the effect of each separate factor should be quantified in the accounts.

60 In addition the profit and loss account or a note thereto should indicate the extent to which the taxation charge for the year has been reduced by accelerated capital allowances, other timing differences and stock   SSAP 15:35

appreciation relief. This means that these individual components should be   Author
separately quantified.

61   Adjustments to the deferred taxation account resulting from a change in the   SSAP 15:36
rate of taxation should be separately disclosed as part of the taxation charge
for the year, unless the change in rate is associated with a fundamental
change in the basis of taxation, in which case the adjustment should be
treated as an extraordinary item.

Dividends

62   The aggregate amount of dividends paid and proposed must be shown in the   1981 1 sch 3(7)(b)
profit and loss account.   SSAP 8:24

63   Dividends must be shown for each class of share, distinguishing between   1981 1 sch 51(3)
dividends already paid and dividends recommended. The rates (per cent or   Author
pence per share) should preferably be stated and it may be helpful to
shareholders to state the date of payment of the dividends.

Redemption of share capital or loans

64   Amounts set aside for redemption of share capital and loans must be   1981 1 sch 53(3)
shown separately.

Earnings Per Share (Listed Companies Only)

Basic earnings per share

65   Earnings per share on the 'net' basis, together with corresponding figures for   SSAP 3:14
the previous year, should be shown on the face of the profit and loss account.

66   Where there is a material difference between earnings per share calculated on   SSAP 3:9
the net basis and on the 'nil distribution' basis, the latter should also be
shown. In this case, 'material' is not defined by the standard, but a difference   Author
in excess of five per cent might be regarded as such.

67   The basis of calculation should be shown either in the profit and loss account   SSAP 3:15
or in a note. Disclosure should include:

(a)   the amount of earnings; and
(b)   the number of equity shares used in the calculation.

Fully diluted earnings per share

68   Fully diluted earnings per share should be shown, in addition to basic   SSAP 3:16
earnings per share, if there are in issue:

(a)   a separate class of equity shares which does not rank for dividend in the
year under review but will do so in the future; or

(b)   debentures, loan stock or preference shares convertible into equity shares of the company; or

(c)   options or warrants to subscribe for equity shares of the company.

However, the fully diluted earnings per share need not be given unless dilution is material. Dilution amounting to five per cent or more is regarded as material for this purpose.   Author

69   Where fully diluted earnings per share are shown: SSAP 3:16

(a)   the basis of calculation of fully diluted earnings per share should be disclosed;

(b)   the corresponding amount for the previous year should not be shown unless the assumptions on which it was based still apply;

(c)   equal prominence should be given to basic and fully diluted earnings per share.

7 Statement of Source and Application of Funds

General

1	All accounts intended to give a true and fair view of the financial position and profit or loss, other than those of enterprises with turnover or gross income of less than £25,000 per annum, should include a statement of source and application of funds for the year under review and for the corresponding previous year.	SSAP 10:9–10

1   All accounts intended to give a true and fair view of the financial position and profit or loss, other than those of enterprises with turnover or gross income of less than £25,000 per annum, should include a statement of source and application of funds for the year under review and for the corresponding previous year.   SSAP 10:9–10

2   In the event that the main accounts are current cost accounts, the statement of source and application of funds should be compatible with the current cost accounts.   SSAP 16:62

3   The statement should show the profit or loss for the year under review together with adjustments required for items which did not use (or provide) funds in the year.   SSAP 10:11

4   The following other sources and applications of funds should, where material, also be shown: SSAP 10:11

(a)   Dividends paid.

(b)   Acquisitions and disposals of fixed and other non-current assets.

(c)   Funds raised by increasing, or expended in repaying or redeeming, medium or long term loans or the issued capital of the company.

(d)   Increase or decrease in working capital, subdivided into its components, and movements in net liquid funds.

Group Accounts

5   Where the accounts are those of a group, the statement of source and application of funds should be so framed as to reflect the operations of the group, and no funds statement need be provided for the holding company.   SSAP 10:12

6   The statement of source and application of funds should reflect any purchase   SSAP 10:5
      or disposal of subsidiary companies either:

      (a)   as separate items; or
      (b)   by showing the effect on the individual items in the statement.

      In the case of acquisitions, it will generally also be necessary to summarise the
      assets acquired, showing how the consideration was provided.

8 Group Accounts

The Legal Requirement for Group Accounts

1 Where at the end of any financial year a company has subsidiaries, 'group accounts' must, where practicable, be laid before the company in general meeting. However, such accounts are not required of a wholly owned subsidiary of another company incorporated in Great Britain. Subsidiaries are defined in Chapter 5.

1948 s 150(1), (2)(a)
SSAP 14:15, 19

2 There is an overriding requirement that group accounts must give a true and fair view of the state of affairs and profit or loss of the holding company and subsidiaries dealt with thereby as a whole, so far as concerns members of the holding company.

1948 s 152(2)–(3)
(introduced by 1981 s 2)

Modified Accounts

3 Companies preparing modified group accounts should refer to Chapter 10, which explains how the rules set out in this chapter are to be modified in their circumstances.

The Form of Group Accounts

4 Group accounts will normally consist of a single set of consolidated accounts comprising:

1948 s 151(1)
SSAP 14:2, 10, 15
1981 1 sch 61

    (a) consolidated balance sheet;
    (b) consolidated profit and loss account;
    (c) consolidated source and application of funds statement; and
    (d) notes on (a), (b) and (c).

Only exceptionally will other forms of group accounts give a better view than consolidated accounts.

5 If, in the opinion of the directors, the members may be better informed thereby, group accounts may be presented as more than one set of consolidated accounts, or in some other form giving equivalent information.

1948 s 151(2)

6   If a group prepares group accounts in a form other than one set of   SSAP 14:22
consolidated accounts in circumstances different from those set out in SSAP
14, the onus is on the directors to justify and state the reasons for reaching the
conclusion that the resulting group accounts give a fairer view of the financial
position of the group as a whole. Similar considerations apply where
consolidated accounts are prepared dealing with a subsidiary which comes
within the scope of the circumstances in which SSAP 14 provides for
exclusion, which are referred to later in this chapter.

7   Group accounts not prepared as consolidated accounts must give the same   1981 1 sch 68
or equivalent information as would have been given had they been
consolidated accounts. Thus, the choice of an unusual method of presenting   Author
the group accounts must not have the incidental effect of reducing the
amount of information disclosed.

8   Group accounts may be wholly or partially incorporated in the holding   1948 s 151(3)
company's accounts.

9   A description should be given of the bases on which subsidiary companies   SSAP 14:15
have been dealt with in the group accounts. A note included to meet this   Author
requirement would normally state whether all subsidiary companies had
been consolidated or, if they had not, would explain the position regarding
subsidiaries not consolidated. Such a note may be included under the
heading 'accounting policies', and confined to a general statement as
indicated above, or the matter may be dealt with in the note giving the
required information about the subsidiary companies.

10   A subsidiary may be omitted from group accounts, if, in the opinion of the   1948 s 150(2)(b)
directors, its inclusion:

   (a)   is impracticable; or

   (b)   would be of no real value to members in view of the insignificant
         amounts involved; or

   (c)   would involve expense or delay disproportionate to the value to
         members; or

   (d)   would be misleading; or

   (e)   would be harmful to the company or its subsidiaries; or

   (f)   is undesirable because the businesses of the holding company and
         subsidiary are so different that they cannot reasonably be treated as a
         single undertaking.

Department of Trade approval is required for omission on the grounds stated in (e) or (f) above.   1948 s 150(2)(b)

11   The directors may decide (with Department of Trade approval where required) that all of the subsidiaries should be excluded from the group accounts for one or more of the reasons set out in the above paragraph. In such circumstances, group accounts are not required.   1948 s 150(2)(b)

12   Subject to the proviso in the next paragraph, the following additional particulars must be stated by note where group accounts are not produced, or subsidiaries are excluded therefrom: 1981 1 sch 69(1)

    (a)   The directors' reasons why subsidiaries are not dealt with in the group accounts.   1981 1 sch 69(2)(a)

    (b)   The aggregate amount of the total investment of the holding company in the shares of subsidiaries calculated under the equity method of valuation. Note that 'equity method of valuation' is not defined, and should be assumed to relate to the determination of the carrying value of the investment that results from the method of accounting contemplated by SSAP 1.   1981 1 sch 69(3)

Author

    (c)   Qualifications in audit reports on the accounts of subsidiaries, or any comment in those accounts calling attention to a matter which, but for that comment, would have been the subject of qualification, where these qualifications: 1981 1 sch 69(2)(b)
       (i)   affect the holding company; and
       (ii)   are not covered by its accounts; and
       (iii)   are material from the point of view of its members.

    (d)   If any of the above information cannot be obtained a statement to that effect should be included instead in the notes.   1981 1 sch 69(5)

The information otherwise required by this paragraph may be omitted or modified if the direction of the Secretary of State is obtained.   1981 1 sch 69(6)

13   The information in (b) of the preceding paragraph is not required if the holding company is itself a wholly owned subsidiary of a body incorporated in Great Britain, and if the directors state in the accounts that in their opinion the value of the investment in subsidiary companies (including indebtedness) is not less than the balance sheet amount.   1981 1 sch 69(4)

14   Where any subsidiary is excluded from group accounts, consideration should be given as to whether group accounts not dealing with one or more   SSAP 14:20

subsidiaries can give a true and fair view of the position of the group as a whole.

15   A holding company need not publish a separate profit and loss account if it: 1948 s 149(5)–(6) (introduced by 1981 s 1(1))

    (a)   publishes a consolidated profit and loss account showing how much of the consolidated profit or loss for the financial year is dealt with in the accounts of the company; and

    (b)   states in a note to the group accounts that advantage has been taken of this dispensation.

In most cases the publication of a separate profit and loss account for a holding company, in addition to a consolidated profit and loss account, is of no real value.   Author

16   Group accounts must be approved by the directors before the balance sheet of the holding company is signed on their behalf.   1948 s 156(2)

Consolidated Accounts

17   Consolidated accounts are defined as a form of group accounts which presents the information contained in the separate accounts of a holding company and its subsidiaries as if they were the accounts of a single entity.   SSAP 14:12

18   Consolidated accounts are to combine the information in the accounts of the holding and subsidiary companies but with such adjustments (if any) as the directors of the holding company think necessary. They must comply with the statutory and other requirements as if the consolidated accounts were the accounts of an actual company.   1981 1 sch 61–62

19   However, in the consolidated accounts the following particulars need be given only in respect of the holding company: 1981 1 sch 63

    (a)   Its directors' emoluments, pensions and compensation for loss of office.   1948 s 196 / 1967 s 6–7

    (b)   Its transactions with directors and other officers.   1980 s 54, 56

    (c)   Certain details of investments in other companies, not being subsidiaries, in accordance with the table set out in Chapter 5.   1967 s 4

    (d)   Employees' emoluments in excess of £20,000 per annum.   1967 s 8

(e) Financial information about subsidiaries and related companies.	1981 s 4

20 It is customary for an analysis of the group's retained profit for the year to be set out below the profit and loss account, showing separately the amounts retained by:

(a) the holding company;	Author
(b) subsidiaries; and	Author
(c) associated companies.	SSAP 1:17

21 If there are significant restrictions on the ability of the holding company to distribute the retained profits of the group (other than those shown as non-distributable) because of statutory, contractual or exchange control restrictions, the extent of the restrictions should be indicated.   SSAP 14:36

Subsidiaries not consolidated

22 SSAP 14 states that a subsidiary should be excluded from consolidation if: SSAP 14:21

(a) its activities are so dissimilar to those of other companies within the group that:
  (i)   consolidated accounts would be misleading; and
  (ii) information for the holding company's shareholders and other users of the statements would be better provided by presenting separate financial statements; or

(b) the holding company, although owning either itself or through other subsidiaries more than half the equity share capital of the subsidiary, either:
  (i)   does not own share capital carrying more than half the votes; or
  (ii) has contractual or other restrictions imposed on its ability to appoint the majority of the board of directors; or

(c) the subsidiary operates under severe restrictions which significantly impair control by the holding company over the subsidiary's assets and operations for the foreseeable future; or

(d) control is intended to be temporary.

The detailed disclosures required in each of the above cases are set out in the next five paragraphs.

23 Where a subsidiary is excluded from consolidation because of dissimilar activities, the group accounts should include separate accounts for that   SSAP 14:23

subsidiary. They may be combined with the accounts of other subsidiaries with similar operations, if appropriate. The separate accounts should include:

(a) a note of the holding company's interest;

(b) particulars of intra group balances;

(c) the nature of transactions with the rest of the group; and

(d) a reconciliation with the amount included in the consolidated accounts for the group's investment in the subsidiary, which should be stated under the equity method of accounting.

24 Where a subsidiary is excluded from consolidation because the holding company does not possess effective control over the votes or the composition of the board, it should be dealt with in the consolidated accounts either: SSAP 14:24

(a) under the equity method of accounting if in all other respects it satisfies the criteria for treatment as an associated company under SSAP 1; or, if these conditions are not met,

(b) as an investment at cost or valuation less any provision required.

In either event, separate financial information about the subsidiary should be included in the group accounts to meet the requirements of the Companies Acts.

25 Where a subsidiary is excluded from consolidation because of severe restrictions which impair control, the amount of the group's investment in the subsidiary should be stated in the consolidated balance sheet at the amount at which it would have been included under the equity method of accounting at the date the restrictions came into force. No further accruals should be made for its profits or losses. However, if the amount at which the investment is stated in the consolidated accounts on this basis has been impaired by a decline in value of the investment (other than temporarily), provision for the loss should be made through the consolidated profit and loss account. For this purpose, investments should be considered individually and not in the aggregate. Where a subsidiary is excluded from consolidation on the above grounds, the following information about that company should be disclosed in the group accounts: SSAP 14:25 SSAP 14:26

(a) Its net assets.
(b) Its profits or losses for the year.

(c) Any amounts included in the consolidated profit and loss account in respect of:
(i) dividends received;
(ii) writing down the investment.

26 Where a subsidiary is excluded from consolidation because control is intended to be temporary, the investment in the subsidiary should be stated in the consolidated balance sheet as a current asset at the lower of cost and net realisable value.   SSAP 14:27

27 Additionally, the following information should be disclosed in the group accounts in respect of all subsidiaries excluded from the consolidated accounts, whatever the reason for their exclusion: SSAP 14:28

(a) The reasons for excluding such subsidiaries from consolidation.

(b) The names of the principal subsidiaries excluded.

(c) Any premium or discount on acquisition (in comparison with the fair value of assets acquired) to the extent not written off.

(d) Any further detailed information required by the Companies Acts.

Minority interests

28 Minority interests in the share capital and reserves of companies consolidated should be shown separately in the consolidated balance sheet. Such items should not be included as part of shareholders' funds. The balance sheet formats do not prescribe where minority interests must be shown, but it is suggested that they follow immediately capital and reserves (in either format) to show that they are neither a liability nor a provision. A debit balance should only be included if the minority is obliged (and able) to make good its share of any losses.   SSAP 14:34   Author   SSAP 14:34

29 The minority interest in the group's results, after taxation and before extraordinary items, should be shown on the face of the profit and loss account. This will mean introducing an extra heading into the standard profit and loss account formats.   SSAP 14:35   Author

30 The 1981 Act is completely silent on the subject of minority interests. It is therefore unclear whether or not the group profit and loss account may deal with extraordinary items net of minority interests. It is suggested that net extraordinary items be shown on the face of the profit and loss account, and the gross amount disclosed by note.

Uniformity of Accounting Policies and Years

31 Uniform group accounting policies should be followed by a holding company in preparing its consolidated accounts. Where such group accounting policies are not adopted in the accounts of a subsidiary, appropriate adjustments should be made in the consolidated accounts. In exceptional cases where this is impracticable, different accounting policies may be used provided they are generally acceptable and there is disclosure of:

 SSAP 14:16

 (a) the different accounting policies used;

 (b) an indication of the amounts of the assets and liabilities involved, and where practicable an indication of the effect on results and net assets of the adoption of policies different from those of the group;

 (c) the reasons for the different treatment.

32 The directors of a holding company must ensure, except where there are good reasons to the contrary, that the financial years of holding and subsidiary companies coincide. Where a subsidiary company or a holding company changes its accounting reference date to coincide with that of the group, this is an exception to the general rule in section 3 of the Companies Act 1976 that accounting reference periods must not be extended until five years have elapsed since any previous extension.

 1948 s 153(1)

 1976 s 3(6)(c)

33 For the purposes of consolidated accounts the accounts of all subsidiaries should wherever practicable be prepared to the same accounting date and for identical accounting periods as those of the holding company. Where the accounting period of a principal subsidiary is of a different length from that of the holding company, the accounting period of the subsidiary should be stated.

 SSAP 14:17

 SSAP 14:18

34 When the financial years of subsidiaries do not coincide with that of the holding company, the accounts of the last financial year ended before the date of the holding company's balance sheet are to be dealt with in the group accounts, unless otherwise permitted by the Secretary of State.

 1948 s 152(4)
 (introduced by 1981 s 2)

35 Where subsidiary companies' accounting periods (whether or not dealt with in any group accounts) are not coterminous with that of the holding company, the notes to the accounts must explain why the directors consider that those subsidiaries' financial years should not end with that of the holding company, and give either the dates of the ends of the subsidiaries' financial years ending last before that of the holding company or the earliest and latest of those year end dates. Additionally, the names of the principal subsidiaries concerned should be stated.

 1981 1 sch 70

 SSAP 14:18

36   Where there have been material additions to, or disposals from, the group,   SSAP 14:30
      the consolidated accounts should contain sufficient information about the
      profits or losses of the subsidiaries acquired or disposed of to enable
      shareholders to understand the effect of the changes on the consolidated
      results.

Investment Companies

37   There are special exemptions available to investment companies preparing   1981 1 sch 74
      consolidated accounts. These are set out in paragraph 74 of the first schedule
      to the Companies Act 1981.

Modification of Statutory Requirements

38   The Department of Trade may, on application, in appropriate cases, modify   1948 s 152(5)
      the requirements of the Act as to the matters to be stated in the group   (introduced by 1981 s 2)
      accounts, provided that the true and fair view is not prejudiced.

9 Current Cost Accounts and the Alternative Accounting Rules

Introduction

1   The Companies Act 1981 specifies two sets of accounting rules. Companies will normally continue to adopt the historical cost accounting rules, but are given the option to adopt instead the alternative accounting rules.

1981 1 sch 29–34

2   The general intent of the legislation is to give statutory support to the concept of providing current cost information in accounts, and to permit the inclusion of certain assets at a valuation in accounts that are in other respects prepared under the historical cost convention.

3   The accounts which a company must prepare to comply with legislation, i.e. its main accounts, may take one of the three following forms:

(a)   Pure historical cost accounts.
(b)   Historical cost accounts incorporating certain asset revaluations.
(c)   Current cost accounts.

4   In addition, the companies to which SSAP 16 applies (see below) will usually attach supplementary accounts, prepared under the current or historical cost conventions, as appropriate. In most cases such companies will prepare their main accounts under the historical cost convention (with or without asset revaluations), with supplementary current cost accounts. However, SSAP 16 also envisages as an alternative the preparation of the main accounts under the current cost convention, with supplementary historical cost accounts. The statutory provisions regarding main accounts do not apply to such supplementary accounts; however, they should have the same general structure as the main accounts in order to aid comparison. Some summarisation is recommended, and in supplementary current cost accounts it may be appropriate to adopt a layout emphasising the relative contributions of loan and equity capital to the financing of the business.

SSAP 16:48

Author

5   If the main accounts are prepared on anything other than a pure historical cost basis, the alternative accounting rules set out in the 1981 Act must be followed. In addition, if the main accounts are current cost accounts, the

1981 1 sch 29–34

provisions of SSAP 16 will also apply. There is a certain overlap between the alternative accounting rules and the requirements of SSAP 16, and so this chapter is divided under three main headings:

(a) Provisions common to SSAP 16 and the alternative accounting rules.
(b) Provisions contained only in the alternative accounting rules.
(c) Provisions contained only in SSAP 16.

Companies should therefore combine such of these provisions as are relevant to their particular circumstances.

Provisions Common to SSAP 16 and the Alternative Accounting Rules

6   Balance sheet items may be valued according to the following rules: SSAP 16:53

(a) Intangible fixed assets, other than goodwill, at current cost.   1981 1 sch 31(1)

(b) Tangible fixed assets at market value at the date of last valuation, or at current cost.   1981 1 sch 31(2)

(c) Stocks at current cost.   1981 1 sch 31(4)

(d) Fixed asset investments at either: 1981 1 sch 31(3)
   (i)   market value on date of last valuation; or
   (ii) a value considered appropriate by the directors, provided that the basis of valuation and the reasons for its adoption are stated.

(e) Assets not covered in (a) to (d) above, stocks not subject to a cost of sales adjustment, and all liabilities on an historical cost basis.

7   The above rules generally specify that assets are to be restated at current cost, whilst SSAP 16 specifies 'value to the business'. In theory these bases of valuation will not always be the same. In practice however there need be no conflict, for two reasons. Firstly, the Act states that assets 'may' rather than 'must' be valued according to the specified rules, and SSAP 16 could therefore legitimately be followed. Secondly, by applying the requirement to make provisions for any permanent diminution in value of fixed assets, current cost, as written down, will normally not be materially different from value to the business.   Author

1981 1 sch 30

1981 1 sch 32

8   The notes must describe the valuation bases and methods adopted, with regard to: 1981 1 sch 33(2)
SSAP 16:58

(a) fixed assets and depreciation;

(b) stocks and work in progress;

(c) current asset investments.

9   Neither the 1981 Act nor SSAP 16 envisages the writing up of goodwill above historical cost.

10   All surpluses (or deficits) arising on restating the historical cost balance sheet onto a current cost basis are to be credited (or. debited) to a 'revaluation reserve' although it need not be called by that name (SSAP 16 prefers 'current cost reserve').

1981 1 sch 34(1), (3)
SSAP 16:54

11   The same accounting principles and policies as adopted in historical cost accounts are to be applied to assets valued according to the alternative accounting rules. For example, stocks are to be included in the balance sheet at the lower of revalued cost and net realisable value.

1981 1 sch 32
SSAP 16:62
Author

Provisions Contained only in the Alternative Accounting Rules

12   Where the balance sheet includes any items on a basis other than historical cost (i.e. at a revalued amount) the following information must be given, either on the face of the balance sheet or in a note to the accounts, in respect of each such balance sheet item (except stocks):

(a) the corresponding historical cost amount and, if relevant, accumulated depreciation; or

1981 1 sch 33(3)–(4)

(b) the difference between the historical cost amount(s) and the amount(s) included in the balance sheet;

1981 1 sch 33(3)(b)

and, except in the case of listed investments,

(c) the years in which the assets were valued and the various values; and

1981 1 sch 43(a)

(d) in the case of assets valued during the year, the names of the valuers or particulars of their qualifications, and the bases of valuation used.

1981 1 sch 43(b)

13   Where the main accounts are current cost accounts, the company may show historical cost depreciation on the face of its profit and loss account, provided that the difference between historical and current cost depreciation (the 'depreciation adjustment') is shown separately, either by note or on the face of the profit and loss account. This will allow companies to provide a reconciliation between the historical cost operating profit and the current cost operating profit on the face of the profit and loss account.

1981 1 sch 32(3)

Author

14   The revaluation reserve must be reduced if the directors consider it no longer necessary for the purpose of the company's accounting policies (e.g. if major fixed assets are disposed of, and are not to be replaced; or if for any

1981 1 sch 34(4)
Author

reason replacement costs decline, perhaps as a result of technological advance). However, in this regard a transfer may only be made to the profit and loss account if either:

(a) the amount was previously charged to that account; or
(b) it represents realised profit.

15   The taxation treatments of items charged or credited to the current cost reserve must be stated. In practice, this will mean stating whether or not any provision for deferred tax has been established in relation to revaluation surpluses.

    1981 1 sch 34(5)
    Author

Provisions Contained only in SSAP 16

16   Current cost accounts are to be included in all accounts intended to show a true and fair view, if the company falls into either of the following categories:

    SSAP 16:46

(a) it is listed on The Stock Exchange; or
(b) at least two of the three following criteria are met:

    (i)   Turnover is more than £5,000,000.
    (ii)   Balance sheet total at the commencement of the accounting year, as shown by the historical cost accounts, is more than £2,500,000.
    (iii) Average number of United Kingdom employees is more than 250.

17   However, notwithstanding the above, current cost accounts are not required if:

    SSAP 16:46

(a) the company is the wholly owned subsidiary of a company registered in the United Kingdom or Eire; or

(b) the company operates as:
    (i)   an authorised insurer; or
    (ii)   a property investment and dealing entity; or
    (iii) a unit trust, investment trust company or similar long term investment entity; or

(c) the primary financial aim of the entity is not to achieve an operating profit.

However, if a holding company which is exempt by virtue of (b) or (c) above has non-exempt subsidiaries, and the non-exempt part of the group exceeds the criteria laid down in subparagraph (b) of the preceding paragraph, then consolidated current cost accounts are required in respect of the non-exempt part of the group.

18 Supplementary current cost accounts should contain a profit and loss   SSAP 16:47, 60–61
account, balance sheet and explanatory notes, together with comparative
figures. Where consolidated current cost statements are produced, and the
holding company's main accounts are historical cost accounts, the holding
company need not produce entity current cost accounts.

19 A current cost profit and loss account should contain the following   SSAP 16:55
information as a minimum:

(a) Current cost operating result.
(b) Interest income attributable to the net borrowing on which the gearing
adjustment has been made.
(c) Gearing adjustment.
(d) Taxation.
(e) Extraordinary items.
(f) Current cost result after tax, attributable to shareholders.

Where current cost accounts are presented as the main accounts, the gearing   Author
adjustment will need to be introduced into the profit and loss account format
adopted.

20 Unless provided on the face of the profit and loss account, a note is required   SSAP 16:56
showing a reconciliation between the historical and current cost operating
profits. This reconciliation should show:

(a) depreciation adjustment;
(b) cost of sales adjustment;
(c) monetary working capital adjustment;
(d) other material adjustments.

The adjustments for cost of sales and monetary working capital may be
combined.

21 Listed companies should state the current cost earnings per share, based on   SSAP 16:59
the attributable current cost profit before extraordinary items.

22 SSAP 16 requires that current asset investments (except those subject to a
cost of sales adjustment) be valued under historical cost principles. Although
the alternative accounting rules permit these assets to be valued at current
cost, the requirements of SSAP 16 should be followed since the adoption of
current cost for these assets is not mandatory under the alternative
accounting rules.

23 Amounts necessary to reduce assets from net current replacement cost to   SSAP 16:54

recoverable amount are to be debited to the profit and loss account, and not to the current cost reserve.

24 The notes to the balance sheet should disclose: SSAP 16:57

 (a) total net operating assets and net borrowing;
 (b) main elements of (a) above;
 (c) summary of movements on fixed assets; and
 (d) a summary of movements on reserves.

25 The notes to the current cost accounts should describe the methods adopted SSAP 16:58
in relation to the following:

 (a) Cost of sales adjustment.
 (b) Monetary working capital adjustment.
 (c) Gearing adjustment.
 (d) Foreign currency translation.
 (e) Other material adjustments.
 (f) Comparative figures.

Investment Properties

26 Compliance with SSAP 19 requires investment properties to be carried in the SSAP 19:11
balance sheet at market value and brings the company within the scope of the
alternative accounting rules. These rules require revalued fixed assets to be 1981 1 sch 32
depreciated, and a conflict therefore arises between the rules and SSAP 19
(which states that the depreciation provisions of SSAP 12 should not be
followed in respect of freehold investment properties).

27 The Accounting Standards Committee (ASC) recommends that companies SSAP 19 part 4
follow SSAP 19 on the grounds that, in the case of investment properties, it is
necessary to depart from the otherwise specific requirement of the law to
provide depreciation on any fixed asset with a limited useful economic life in
order to comply with the overriding requirement for the accounts to give a
true and fair view. Where the ASC recommendation is followed, the directors 1948 s 149(4)
must give, in a note to the accounts, particulars of the departure, the reasons (introduced by 1981 s
for it, and its effect. 1(1))

Investment Companies

28 Investment companies are exempted from some of the applications of the 1981 1 sch 71(1)
alternative accounting rules. Details are given in the first schedule to the
Companies Act 1981.

10 The Accounting Exemptions

Publication

1   Reference is made in this chapter to companies 'publishing' accounts. A company will be deemed to have published accounts if it publishes, issues or circulates them or otherwise makes them available for public inspection in a manner calculated to invite members of the public generally, or any class of members of the public, to read them, for example by publishing a preliminary announcement.   1981 s 21(3)

Full Accounts

2   The accounts, whether individual or group accounts, which are required to be prepared and laid before the shareholders are called 'full accounts'. When applying the rules relating to publication of accounts the term full accounts also includes modified accounts, which are those accounts taking advantage of the accounting exemptions for small and medium sized companies, as explained below.   1981 s 11(2), (5)

3   Where a company which is required to prepare group accounts publishes individual accounts it must also publish with those accounts the group accounts. These group accounts may be in modified form if the individual accounts published are also in modified form.   1981 s 11(3)

4   Where a company publishes full individual or group accounts it must publish with those accounts the relevant auditors' report.   1981 s 11(1), (4)

Abridged Accounts

5   Where a company publishes abridged accounts (i.e. any profit and loss account or balance sheet other than those included in full accounts) it must publish with those accounts a statement indicating: 1981 s 11(6), (8)

(a)   that the accounts are not full accounts; and

(b)   whether full accounts have been delivered to the registrar of companies; and

(c) whether an auditors' report has been given on any accounts relating to the financial year covered by the abridged accounts; and

(d) whether any such auditors' report was unqualified. Where such a report is qualified, it might be regarded as good practice to outline the nature and extent of the qualification.   Author

A company publishing abridged accounts is not permitted to publish with those accounts the auditors' report on the full accounts.   1981 s 11(7), (9)

Accounting Exemptions for the Preparation of Modified Accounts

General

6   The accounting exemptions are available to certain small and medium sized companies. To be classified as small or medium sized, as the case may be, a company or group of companies must meet at least two out of the following three criteria: 1981 s 8(1)–(3)

	Small	*Medium sized*
(a) Annual turnover not exceeding	£1,400,000	£5,750,000
(b) Balance sheet total not exceeding	£700,000	£2,800,000
(c) Average number of employees not exceeding	50	250

7   Balance sheet total is the aggregate of items A to D in format 1 or the aggregate of amounts shown under the general heading 'Assets' in format 2.   1981 s 8(9)

8   If a company qualifies to be classed as small or medium sized in any year, and is accordingly entitled to the accounting exemptions for that year, it will also be entitled to the same exemptions in the following year, regardless of whether or not it meets the criteria in that following year.   1981 s 8(5)

9   A company failing to so qualify in two successive years will cease to be entitled to the accounting exemptions for the second year in which it fails to meet the relevant criteria.   1981 s 8(6)

10   Transitional provisions permit a company to take advantage of the exemptions in the year in which the accounting exemptions first become effective, if the company qualifies under the terms set out above in that year or in the previous year.   1981 s 8(8)

11   The accounting exemption provisions permit small and medium sized companies to file with the registrar of companies an abbreviated form of annual accounts. These accounts, officially referred to as modified accounts,   1981 s 5(1), 6(1)

are an abbreviated form of the full statutory accounts which companies are required to prepare and lay before their shareholders. The opportunity to file or publish modified accounts in no way affects the requirement to prepare full accounts for the shareholders. The accounting exemptions thus do not provide any relief for small or medium sized companies from preparing full accounts and, if advantage is taken of the accounting exemptions, additional time and expense will be incurred in preparing modified accounts, which also require a special auditors' report. The only advantage to be gained from modified accounts is therefore a degree of confidentiality since certain information which might be of interest to competitors (profit margin, sales analyses etc) can be omitted from such accounts.

Author

Eligibility

12 The accounting exemptions are available to companies or groups which qualify as small or medium sized. However, a company will not be entitled to the exemptions, regardless of its size, if it is:

1981 s 5(3)

(a) a public company; or
(b) a banking, insurance or shipping company (as defined in the introduction to this book); or
(c) a member of an ineligible group.

13 An ineligible group is a holding company and its subsidiaries, any member of which is:

1981 s 5(4)–(5)

(a) a public company; or
(b) a banking, insurance or shipping company; or
(c) a body corporate (other than a company) which has power to offer shares or debentures to the public; or
(d) a body corporate (other than a company) which is either a recognised bank or a licensed deposit taker, or an insurance company.

Small company exemptions

14 A company qualifying to be treated as small is entitled to the following accounting exemptions:

1981 s 6(2)

(a) It need not file a profit and loss account.   1981 s 6(2)(b)
(b) It need not file a directors' report.   1981 s 6(6)
(c) It may file a modified balance sheet.   1981 s 6(2)(a)
(d) Certain information normally required to be given in the notes to the accounts may be omitted.   1981 s 6(2)(c)–(d)

15 The modified balance sheet need include only those headings in the standard formats marked with Roman numerals. For debtors and creditors separate

1981 s 6(3)–(4)

totals must be shown, either on the balance sheet or in the notes to the accounts, of aggregate amounts falling due before and after one year.

16   The notes to the accounts need only include the following information   1981 s 6(5)
required by the first schedule to the Companies Act 1981:

(a)   Accounting policies.
(b)   Share capital.
(c)   Particulars of allotments.
(d)   Particulars of debts.
(e)   Basis of translation of foreign currencies.
(f)   Corresponding amounts for previous financial year.

It should be emphasised that these exemptions are confined to the disclosure   Author
requirements contained in the first schedule to the Companies Act 1981.
Therefore, in general, the other statutory requirements must still be met.
However, the notes to the accounts need not include the information on: 1981 s 6(2)(d)

(g)   directors' emoluments etc, as required by section 196 of the Companies
Act 1948 (see Chapter 6);
(h)   directors' and certain other employees' emoluments etc, as required by
sections 6, 7 and 8 of the Companies Act 1967 (see Chapter 6).

Since modified accounts are not intended to give a true and fair view, it will   Author
not be necessary for such accounts to comply with the disclosure provisions
of SSAPs.

Medium sized company exemptions

17   A company qualifying to be treated as medium sized is entitled to file a   1981 s 6(7)(a)–(b)
modified profit and loss account. The normal requirements for full directors'
report, balance sheet and notes to the accounts are not affected, except that
details of turnover are not required to be given in the notes to the accounts.

18   A modified profit and loss account will be as set out in the standard formats   1981 s 6(8)
subject to combining as one item, under the heading 'Gross profit or loss':

(a)   items 1, 2, 3 and 6 in format 1;
(b)   items 1 to 5 in format 2;
(c)   items A1, B1 and B2 in format 3;
(d)   items A1, A2 and B1 to B4 in format 4.

Directors' responsibilities

19   Where modified accounts are filed, they must be signed by at least two   1981 s 7(1)
directors, or if there is only one director, by that director.

20   Immediately above the signature of the directors there must be included a   1981 s 7(2)–(3)
      statement by the directors that they have relied upon the exemptions for
      individual accounts on the grounds that the company is entitled to do so as a
      small or a medium sized company (and stating which).

Auditors' responsibility

21   Where modified accounts are filed there must be included a report by the   1981 s 7(4)
      auditors:

      (a)   stating that in their opinion the conditions for exemption have been met;   1981 s 7(5)(a)
             and

      (b)   reproducing the full text of their report on the accounts prepared for the   1981 s 7(5)(b)
             shareholders.

Group exemption

22   Where group accounts are required to be prepared, the accounting   1981 s 9(1), 10(1)–(2)
      exemptions permit modified accounts to be filed both for the holding
      company and for the group.

23   In deciding whether a group meets the size criteria for the accounting   1981 s 9(4)–(6)
      exemptions, i.e. whether it is small or medium sized, a consolidation of all
      subsidiaries must be used.

24   A holding company may only file modified individual accounts if the group of   1981 s 9(2)
      which it is the holding company would also qualify to be treated as small or
      medium sized.

25   Where a group would qualify as medium sized the holding company must   1981 s 9(3)
      also be treated as medium sized for the purpose of the accounting
      exemptions, even though, alone, it meets the normal criteria for a small
      company.

26   Modified group accounts may only be filed if the holding company is entitled   1981 s 10(2)
      to, and has taken advantage of, the accounting exemptions by itself filing
      modified accounts.

27   Where modified group accounts are filed, the directors' statement concerning   1981 s 10(5)
      eligibility to file modified accounts made on the holding company's balance
      sheet must include a statement that modified group accounts will be filed at
      the same time.

Dormant Companies

28   A company is regarded as dormant if during any period there were no   1981 s 12(6)
      accounting transactions required to be entered in the accounting records.

Transactions arising from the initial issue of shares to the subscribers to the memorandum may be ignored for this purpose.

29   A company, other than one required to prepare group accounts, may by special resolution decide not to appoint auditors, provided that either: 1981 s 12(1)–(5), (9)

(a)   the company has remained dormant since its incorporation; or

(b)   (i)   it meets the small or medium sized company criteria set out in the accounting exemption rules, notwithstanding that it is a member of an ineligible group; and

(ii)   it has been dormant since the end of the previous financial year.

30   There must be included in the unaudited balance sheet of a dormant company filed with the registrar, a statement by the directors to the effect that the company was dormant throughout the period covered by the accounts. 1981 s 12(10)–(11)

11 Company Records and Regulations

Introduction

1   This chapter sets out some important aspects of company law, The Stock Exchange Listing Agreement and other regulations, some of which are not directly concerned with accounts disclosure but of which the preparer or auditor of accounts should be aware.

Accounting Records and Statutory Books

Nature of records

2   It is the duty of the company to keep accounting records which are sufficient to show and explain the company's transactions and are such as to: 1976 s 12(2)

    (a) disclose with reasonable accuracy, at any time, the financial position of the company at that time; and   1976 s 12(3)(a)

    (b) enable the directors to ensure that any balance sheet or profit and loss account prepared by them in accordance with section 1 of the Companies Act 1976 complies with the requirements of section 149 of the Companies Act 1948 (introduced by section 1 of the Companies Act 1981) (accounts to give a true and fair view and comply with disclosure requirements).   1976 s 12(3)(b)

3   The accounting records must in particular contain:

    (a) entries from day to day of all sums of money received and expended, and the matters in respect of which the receipt and expenditure take place;   1976 s 12(4)(a)

    (b) a record of assets and liabilities; and   1976 s 12(4)(b)

    (c) where the company's business involves dealing in goods, statements of stocks held by the company at the end of each financial year. The company must retain all statements of stocktakings from which the statements of stocks are prepared and, except in the case of goods sold   1976 s 12(4)(c), (5) by way of ordinary retail trade, records of goods sold and purchased identifying the goods and the buyers and sellers.

4   Accounts and returns must be sent to Great Britain in respect of accounting records kept outside Great Britain and must be such as to: 1976 s 12(8)

    (a) disclose with reasonable accuracy the financial position of the business in question at intervals not exceeding six months; and

    (b) enable the directors to prepare accounts which comply with section 149 of the Companies Act 1948, as introduced by section 1 of the 1981 Act.

Retention of records

5   The accounting records described above must be kept, in the case of a private company, for three years from the date on which they are made and, in any other case, for six years from the date on which they are made. The retention period stated in the Act should be regarded as a minimum. Other considerations (e.g. prospectus requirements, Statute of Limitation, Inland Revenue and VAT enquiries) may also need to be taken into account.   1976 s 12(9)

Author

Form of records

6   A register, index, minute book or accounting record may be kept in a bound book or otherwise.   1948 s 436

Statutory books

7   The books to be kept and their location are set out below:

Statutory books	*To be kept at*	
(a) Register of directors and secretaries. Every company must have a secretary and, unless a private company, at least two directors. The statement of first directors and secretary and changes thereto is to be notified to the registrar of companies.	Registered office.	1948 s 176–177, 200 1976 s 21(1), 22(1)
(b) Register of charges and copies of all instruments creating such charges.	Registered office.	1948 s 103–104 1948 s 106(H)–(I)
(c) Minute books of general meeting.	Registered office.	1948 s 146
(d) Minute books of meetings of directors or managers.	No requirements.	1948 s 145
(e) Register of members and, where required, index thereto.	Registered office or such other place as may be notified to the registrar of companies.	1948 s 110–111

Statutory books	*To be kept at*	
(f) Register of debenture holders.	Registered office or such other place as may be notified to the registrar of companies.	1948 s 86
(g) Register of directors' interests in shares and debentures of group companies.	Registered office or place at which register of members is kept. Registrar to be notified of place kept if other than registered office.	1967 s 29
(h) Register of persons, or persons acting together, interested in 5 per cent or more of the share capital of the company.	Wherever the register of directors' interests is kept.	1981 s 73

8   Notice of any change in the situation of a company's registered office must be given to the registrar of companies within 14 days of the change.   1976 s 23(3)

Annual Return

9   Every company having a share capital must submit an annual return at least once in each year. However, no return is required in the year of incorporation, or in the following year, if no annual general meeting needs to be held. The annual return must contain the following information: 1948 s 124

1948 6 sch part I

(a) The address of the registered office.
(b) The locations of registers of members and debenture holders, if not kept at the registered office.
(c) Full details of the company's share capital.
(d) Total indebtedness in respect of all mortgages and charges.
(e) A list of members and their holdings.
(f) Details of the company's secretary and directors.

A full list of shareholders is required only every third year. In other years, a list of changes in membership and holdings will suffice.   1948 s 124(1)(c)

10   There are different provisions relating to the annual returns of companies having Dominion registers, and those having no share capital. These are contained in the Companies Act 1948.   1948 s 124(2), 125

11   The annual return must be completed within 42 days after the annual general meeting, and must be filed with the registrar immediately. The return must be signed by a director and by the company secretary.   1948 s 126

Regulations Concerning Directors

Directors' service contracts

12   For each director of the company who is employed under a service contract with either the company or any of its subsidiaries, there must be kept available for inspection by the members during reasonable business hours a copy of the contract. If the contract is not in writing, or if the director is required to work wholly or mainly outside the United Kingdom, a written memorandum of the terms of the contract will suffice.

1967 s 26(1), (3A)
1980 s 61(1)–(2)

13   The location of these documents, which may be the registered office, the principal place of business or the place where the register of members is kept, must be notified to the registrar.

1967 s 26(2)–(3)

14   No copy or memorandum of a director's service contract is required to be made available if the contract has less than 12 months to run, or may be terminated by the company within the next 12 months without payment of compensation.

1967 s 26(8)(b)

Directors' qualification shares

15   The number of qualification shares as specified by the articles must be acquired within two months, or such period as is stated by the articles if less. Qualification shares cannot consist of bearer shares.

1948 s 182

Directors' age limit

16   Subject to the exceptions in the following paragraph:

(a)   no person may be appointed a director of a company if, at the time of the appointment, he has reached the age of 70; and

1948 s 185(1)

(b)   a director shall vacate office (and shall be ineligible for reelection) at the conclusion of the annual general meeting next after he reaches the age of 70.

1948 s 185(2)

17   The above provisions do not apply if:

(a)   the appointment is made or approved by the company in general meeting and special notice (section 142 of the Companies Act 1948), stating the age of the person concerned, has been given; or

1948 s 185(5)

(b)   there are provisions to the contrary in the company's articles; or

1948 s 185(7)

(c)   the company is a private company, not being the subsidiary of a public company incorporated in the United Kingdom.

1948 s 185(8)

18   A person who is proposed or appointed as a director of a company subject to these provisions must give notice of his age to the company, if at that date he has reached the age of 70 or any other retiring age specified by the articles.   1948 s 186

Secretarial Matters

European Communities Act 1972

19   Business letters and order forms must show: European Communities Act 1972 s 9

(a)   the place of registration;
(b)   the company's registered number; and
(c)   the address of the registered office.

If such documents refer to the share capital of the company, this must be the paid up capital. The fact that a company is limited must also be stated, even if the company is authorised under section 25 of the Companies Act 1981 to omit the word 'limited' from its name.

20   Business letters on which the company's name appears must not state the name of any of its directors (otherwise than in the text or as a signatory) unless the letter states the names of all individual or corporate directors of the company.   1948 s 201(1A) (introduced by 1981 3 sch 11)

21   An up to date version of the company's memorandum and articles must be filed with the registrar. Any alterations to either document must be printed. Where the amendments are minor the registrar allows, by concession, amendment slips to be inserted, provided these obscure the amended words.   European Communities Act 1972 s 9(5) Author

Accounting Reference Date and Accounts

22   The directors must prepare a profit and loss account for each accounting reference period ending within seven days either side of the accounting reference date, and a balance sheet as at the date up to which the profit and loss account is prepared together with appropriate notes. A copy of these items together with the auditors' and directors' reports must be delivered to the registrar of companies within 10 months of the accounting reference date (for private companies) or within seven months of the accounting reference date (for other companies). In either case: 1976 s 1(1)–(4)

    1976 s 6(2)

(a)   the period will be reduced if a first accounting period is more than 12 months; and   1976 s 6(4)

(b)   the period can be extended by three months where the company carries on business, or has interests, outside the United Kingdom, providing notice is given to the registrar.   1976 s 6(3)

23   A company must notify the registrar of companies of its accounting reference   1976 s 2(1)–(3), 3
date and changes thereto. If no such notice is given, the reference date will be
deemed to be 31 March.

24   The balance sheet must be signed by two directors or, if there is only one   1948 s 155(1)
director, by that director. It is not wholly clear (as a result of paragraph 62 of   Author
the first schedule to the 1981 Act) whether there is a legal requirement for the
consolidated balance sheet to be signed in the same way, but in any event this
procedure is regarded as good practice.

25   The balance sheet, profit and loss account, notes and other documents   1948 s 156(2)
required to be annexed thereto must be approved by the board before the
balance sheet is signed. The accounts should disclose the date of their   SSAP 17:26
approval.

General Meetings

26   A company must hold its first annual general meeting within 18 months of   1948 s 131
incorporation, and subsequently once in each calendar year but not more   1976 s 1(6)
than 15 months after the date of the previous general meeting. Accounts are
to be laid before members in general meeting (usually, but not necessarily, the
annual general meeting).

27   Accounts must be circulated not less than 21 days before the general meeting   1948 s 158
before which they are to be laid, to every member and debenture holder and
also to any other person who is entitled to receive notice of general meetings.
If all members entitled to attend and vote at the meeting agree, notice may be
waived.

28   The accounts to be circulated consist of, as a minimum, the balance sheet and   1948 s 156(1), 157(1)
profit and loss account and notes, together with the auditors' and directors'   1967 s 24
reports.

29   The notice convening the annual general meeting of a listed company is to   LA para 11(b)–(c)
state that there will be made available for inspection at the registered office,
or transfer office, from the date of the notice to the date of the meeting and at
the meeting, copies of, or written memoranda of the terms of, all directors'
service contracts with the company or any subsidiary (unless the contract of
service is expiring, or determinable by the company without payment of
compensation, within one year). If there are no contracts, that fact is to be
stated in the notice. However, no company may approve a director's service   1980 s 47(4)
contract unless a memorandum of the proposed terms was available at the
general meeting itself, and at the registered office for the 15 preceding days.

Interim and Preliminary Announcements

30   For listed companies a half yearly report is to be circulated to shareholders   LA para 9
and debenture holders, or inserted as a paid advertisement in two leading
daily newspapers, not later than six months from the date of the notice
convening the annual general meeting. It should contain similar information
to that required in a preliminary announcement of results. In the case of the   USM 8:4
USM, the advertisement need only be circulated to shareholders or
published in one newspaper.

31   In the absence of any special circumstances, the following minimum   ASL sch VII part C
information should be included when preliminary announcements in respect
of any year, half year or other accounting period or part thereof are made. In
the case of a holding company, the information should be given in respect of
the group. Figures which are provisional or subject to audit should be so
qualified. The particulars required are:

     (a)   Historical cost information:
         (i)   Turnover.
         (ii)   Profit (or loss) after all charges, including taxation.
         (iii)   United Kingdom and, where material, overseas taxation charged
               in arriving at (ii).
         (iv)   For groups only, profit attributable to members of holding
               company, and to minority interests.
         (v)   Extraordinary items, net of taxation.
         (vi)   Rates of dividend(s) paid and proposed and the amount absorbed
               thereby.
         (vii)   Earnings per share expressed as pence per share.
         (viii) Comparative figures for (i) to (vii) above for the corresponding
               previous period.
         (ix)   Any supplementary information which in the opinion of the
               directors is necessary for a reasonable appreciation of the results.

     (b)   Current cost information (if required):
         (i)   The current cost operating profit or loss.
         (ii)   Interest/income relating to the net borrowing on which the
               gearing adjustment has been based.
         (iii)   The gearing adjustment.
         (iv)   Taxation.
         (v)   Current cost profit or loss (after tax) attributable to members of
               the (holding) company, i.e. after deduction of minority interests.
         (vi)   The amounts of the current cost operating adjustments.
         (vii)   Current cost earnings per share.

    (viii) Corresponding figures for the preceding period.

    (ix)   Any supplementary information which, in the opinion of the directors, is necessary for a reasonable appreciation of the current cost results of the year including, if material, the extent to which (b)(v) above has been affected by special credits and/or debits.

It should be noted that any such announcement will constitute the publication of abridged accounts. The relevant statutory provisions set out in Chapter 10 must be followed.   Author

Sundry Matters — Listed Companies

32   Listed companies are recommended by a letter from the chairman of The Stock Exchange to disclose in the annual report: The Stock Exchange

    (a)   a table of relevant comparative figures for the past 10 years. In practice a table for five years is acceptable and may, because of inflation, be preferable;   Author

    (b)   a list of principal products.

Types of Company

Public companies

33   A public company is one which fulfils the following requirements: 1980 s 1(1)

    (a)   It must be limited by shares or be limited by guarantee and have a share capital, although no company in the latter category may be newly formed as a public company.

    (b)   Its memorandum of association must state that it is to be a public company.

    (c)   The provisions of the Companies Acts in relation to the registration of such a company must be fulfilled.

    (d)   It must have not less than two members and two directors.   1980 s 2(1)
1948 s 176

    (e)   Its name must end with the words 'public limited company' or 'plc' or, in the case of a company whose registered office is in Wales, those words, initials or their equivalent in Welsh.   1980 s 2(2), 78

    (f)   It must have a minimum allotted share capital of £50,000.   1980 s 4(2), 85(1)

Private companies

34   A private company is any company which is not a public company. Such companies will therefore include all unlimited companies, and all companies limited by guarantee which do not have a share capital. A private company has the following privileges: 1980 s 1(1)

(a)   The minimum number of directors is one, but a sole director cannot also hold the office of secretary.   1948 s 176

(b)   The provision regarding the age limit of directors does not apply, provided the company is not a subsidiary of a public company incorporated in the United Kingdom.   1948 s 185

(c)   When authorised to purchase or redeem its own shares, a private company may do so out of capital, rather than only out of distributable profits.   1981 s 54

(d)   It may more readily give financial assistance for the purchase of its own, or its holding company's, shares.   1981 s 43

(e)   Less strict criteria apply in the determination of distributable profits.   1980 s 39–40

However, a private company is prohibited from offering its shares or debentures to the public.   1980 s 15

Unlimited companies

35   An unlimited company incorporated under the Companies Acts is subject to the same disclosure requirements as a limited company. However, an unlimited company is not required to file its accounts, auditors' or directors' reports with its annual return provided that, at no time during the accounting reference period, was it: 1976 s 1(8)

(a)   the subsidiary of a limited company; or
(b)   the holding company of a limited company; or
(c)   carrying on business within the meaning of the Trading Stamps Act 1964.

Oversea companies

36   Oversea companies are defined as companies incorporated outside Great Britain which have a place of business in Great Britain. Companies incorporated in the Channel Islands or the Isle of Man are treated for the purposes of the Acts as if they were registered in England or Scotland.   1948 s 406, 416

37   An oversea company must in respect of every accounting reference period prepare accounts substantially in the form that would have been required   1976 s 9

had the company been incorporated under the Act. The available exemptions are set out in the following paragraph. There is no requirement that such documents must be circulated to shareholders, but copies must be delivered to the registrar of companies, together with a certified translation thereof where they are not written in the English language. The period allowed for delivery to the registrar is 13 months from the accounting reference date.

1976 s 11(2)

38   The exemptions referred to above allow oversea companies to omit the following from their accounts:

SI 1980 No 1786

(a)   Auditors' report.
(b)   Directors' report.
(c)   Details of subsidiaries and investments.
(d)   Identity of ultimate holding company.
(e)   Details of directors' and employees' emoluments.

In addition, such companies need not apply section 56 of the 1948 Act (creation of share premium account).

39   If the Secretary of State serves notice on an oversea company that its corporate name is undesirable as a business name, such company must, if it wishes to continue in business in Great Britain, thereupon adopt another name, approved by the Secretary of State, as its business name, and that other name must be notified to the registrar of companies.

1976 s 31
(amended by 1981 s 27)

12 Provisions Affecting Capital and Distributions

Introduction

1 This chapter sets out certain of the legal requirements concerning capital and distributions which, although not directly related to disclosure, are relevant to the production of annual accounts. The provisions included relate to:

(a) the purchase by a company of its own shares;
(b) financial assistance for acquisition of shares;
(c) share premiums; and
(d) distributions of profits and assets.

These matters are dealt with in this book either because the legislation was introduced by the Companies Act 1981, or because that Act modified provisions in earlier Acts.

2 These particular topics are complex, and this chapter does not set out to be comprehensive. In cases of doubt, reference should always be made to the legislation, and in difficult cases it is recommended that appropriate legal advice is obtained.

The Purchase by a Company of its Own Shares

3 A company, if empowered by its Articles, may purchase its own shares (whether or not these shares are designated as redeemable) provided that, after any purchase, non-redeemable shares are still in issue.

1981 s 46(1)

1981 s 46(3)

4 A purchase may be made from:

1981 s 45(5), 46(2)

(a) the proceeds of an issue made for that purpose; and/or
(b) distributable profits.

Any premium payable on purchase must be paid out of distributable profits, except where the purchase is of shares originally issued at a premium when, with certain limits (see below), the premium may be paid out of the proceeds of an issue for that purpose.

5   A public company may only purchase its own shares from the above sources. However, a private company may also make purchases out of capital (see below).

6   Shares purchased are treated as cancelled and the nominal value of the issued share capital is reduced accordingly. Where a purchase is made wholly out of distributable profits an amount equal to the reduction of the issued share capital is required to be transferred to a capital redemption reserve. This reserve may thereafter only be applied for a bonus issue of new capital.

1981 s 45(8), 46(2)
1981 s 53(1), (3)

7   Where a purchase of shares is made wholly or partly out of a fresh issue of shares and the proceeds of this issue are less than the aggregate nominal value of shares purchased the difference must be transferred to a capital redemption reserve.

1981 s 53(2)

8   Where the shares being purchased were themselves issued at a premium, any premium payable on the purchase may be paid out of the proceeds of a fresh issue made for that purpose and the share premium account reduced accordingly by an amount up to the lower of:

1981 s 45(6), 46(2)

(a)   the current amount of share premium account including the amount of the premium on the new issue transferred to it; and

(b)   the aggregate of the premiums received on the issue of the shares being purchased.

9   The following further provisions apply to purchase of own shares:

(a)   The shares to be purchased must be fully paid.

1981 s 45(3), 46(2)

(b)   The purchase terms must provide for payment on purchase.

1981 s 45(4), 46(2)

(c)   The authorised share capital is not reduced by the purchase. However, if a company is about to purchase its own shares out of a new issue, it can issue new shares up to the nominal amount of the shares purchased as if the original shares had never been issued and so not exceed its authorised capital.

1981 s 45(8)–(9)
1981 s 46(2)

Purchase out of capital

10   In addition to being able to purchase its own shares out of distributable profits and the proceeds of a new issue, a private company is allowed to purchase shares out of capital, but only if:

1981 s 54(1)

(a)   it provides the safeguards for creditors set out below; and
(b)   it is empowered to do so by its Articles.

11   The payment which may be made out of capital is referred to as the   1981 s 54(2)–(3)
      'permissible capital payment'. The permissible capital payment is the cost of
      purchase of the shares less:

      (a)   any available profits of the company; and

      (b)   the proceeds of any fresh issue made for the purpose of the redemption
            or purchase.

      The available profits for this purpose are the profits out of which a   1981 s 54(7)–(10)
      distribution could be made under the 1980 Act as shown by the 'relevant
      accounts' (see below) prepared as at a date within three months ending on
      the date on which the statutory declaration of the directors (see below) is
      made.

12   The effect of these provisions is that the purchase of own shares will result in a
      depletion of capital only to the extent that the distributable profits and/or the
      proceeds of a fresh issue are inadequate. However, subject to the requirement
      for a private company to have two members, with at least one member
      holding non-redeemable shares, there would appear to be no limit to the
      extent to which such a company may purchase its own shares.

13   If the permissible capital payment, which includes for this purpose the
      proceeds of any new issue applied in making the purchase:

      (a)   is less than the nominal value of the shares purchased the difference must   1981 s 54(4), (6)
            be transferred to the capital redemption reserve; or

      (b)   exceeds the nominal value of the shares purchased the following may be   1981 s 54(5)–(6)
            reduced by the excess:
            (i)   the capital redemption reserve, the share premium account or fully
                   paid share capital; and
            (ii)   unrealised profits included in the revaluation reserve maintained
                   under paragraph 34 of the first schedule to the 1981 Act.

14   The safeguards for creditors are as follows:

      (a)   The directors must make and file with the registrar a statutory   1981 s 55(3)–(4)
            declaration, in the prescribed form, that after making full enquiry they
            are of the opinion that after making the capital payment:
            (i)   there will be no grounds on which the company could be found
                   unable to pay its debts; and

    (ii)   the company will be able to continue as a going concern, paying its debts as they fall due, for the next 12 months.

(b)   The statutory declaration must have annexed to it a report by the auditors of the company to the directors stating that the amount of the permissible capital payment has been properly determined, and that having enquired into the company's state of affairs they are not aware of anything to indicate that the directors' opinion is unreasonable in all the circumstances.   1981 s 55(5)

(c)   Payments out of capital must be approved by special resolution. The members holding shares to which the resolution relates cannot exercise the voting rights carried by those shares if this exercise would be necessary to enable the resolution to be passed.   1981 s 55(2), (7)

(d)   The special resolution must be passed within a week of the statutory declaration, and the payment out of capital cannot be earlier than five or later than seven weeks after the date of the resolution.   1981 s 55(6)

(e)   Within a week following the date of the resolution the company must publish a notice giving specified information in the Gazette and also either publish the same notice in an appropriate national newspaper or send the information to each of its creditors.   1981 s 56(1)–(2)

(f)   The statutory declaration together with the report of the auditors thereon must be filed with the registrar not later than the day on which the first notice under (e) above is published, and must be available for inspection at the registered office.   1981 s 56(4)–(5)

(g)   Within five weeks of the date of the resolution any creditor or any member of the company who did not consent to or vote in favour of the payment may apply to the court to have the resolution cancelled. The court may make an order on such terms as it thinks fit, either confirming or cancelling the resolution.   1981 s 57

(h)   If a company is wound up within a year of making a purchase out of capital, the directors who signed the statutory declaration and the members from whom the shares were purchased may become liable to meet any insufficiency of assets up to the amount paid out of capital on the purchase.   1981 s 58

Authorisation of purchases by members

15   The purchase of a company's own shares on The Stock Exchange must be authorised by a resolution in general meeting: 1981 s 49

(a) specifying the maximum number of shares to be acquired;

(b) determining the maximum and minimum prices that may be paid for those shares; and

(c) specifying a date not more than 18 months in advance upon which the authority is to expire.

16 Where a company wishes to purchase its own shares otherwise than on The Stock Exchange it must obtain a special resolution approving the proposed off-market purchase contract. This approval procedure is subject to the following safeguards: **1981 s 47(5)**

(a) The members holding shares to which the resolution relates cannot exercise the voting rights carried by those shares if their exercise would be necessary to enable the resolution to be passed. **1981 s 47(9)**

(b) The proposed purchase contract must be available for inspection by the members at the registered office for the 15 days preceding the meeting and at the meeting itself. **1981 s 47(10)**

(c) In the case of public companies, the resolution must specify a date, not more than 18 months in advance, by which the authority conferred will expire. **1981 s 47(7), (8)**

Filing and inspection requirements

17 Details of every purchase must be filed with the registrar within 28 days. In addition, companies are required to keep available for public inspection at their registered office details of contracts of purchase of own shares for 10 years after each purchase. **1981 s 52(1), (4)**

Redeemable shares

18 Companies may issue redeemable equity shares provided that non-redeemable shares are also in issue. The rules that govern the redemption of redeemable shares are similar to those for the purchase of own shares. Companies' Articles may include any redemption terms that do not conflict with the requirements of the Act. **1981 s 45(1)**

1981 s 45(7)

Financial Assistance for Acquisition of Shares

19 Subject to the exemptions set out below companies cannot give, either directly or indirectly, financial assistance for the purpose of the acquisition of their own shares or the shares of their holding company. This applies to financial assistance given: **1981 s 42**

(a)   both before or at the same time as the acquisition; or   1981 s 42(1)

(b)   by means of reducing or discharging after acquisition a liability incurred   1981 s 42(2)
by any person for the purpose of the acquisition.

20   The above provisions do not prohibit: 1981 s 42(6)

(a)   the lending of money by a company in the ordinary course of its
business; or

(b)   the acquisition of fully paid shares under an employee share scheme; or

(c)   loans to employees (who are not directors) to enable them to acquire
beneficial ownership of fully paid shares in the company;

provided in the case of a public company that it has net assets which   1981 s 42(7)
are not thereby reduced or the reduction is provided out of distributable
profits.

21   Normally, giving financial assistance by these means would not result in any
reduction in net assets. It is believed that this requirement has been
introduced to prevent financial assistance being given with the intention that
the resultant debt will not be collected.

22   The prohibition does not apply if the company's principal purpose in giving   1981 s 42(3)–(4)
financial assistance is not to give it for the purpose of acquisition of shares, or
the assistance given is an incidental part of some larger purpose of the
company, and the assistance is given in good faith and in the interests of the
company.

23   It is understood that this provision has been included because the words
'financial assistance for the purpose of or in connection with the acquisition
of shares' in the 1948 Act were interpreted narrowly by the courts. Under the
new provisions it now seems that if, for example, a subsidiary is acquired and
that subsidiary proceeds to guarantee the borrowings of the holding
company as part of a prior contractual arrangement (e.g. contained in the
holding company's debenture stock trust deed) that subsidiary would not be
regarded as providing financial assistance for the purpose of the acquisition
of its shares. However, care will be needed in interpreting this provision, and
legal advice should be obtained where necessary.

24   The above provisions do not prohibit the following, although they may   1981 s 42(5)
effectively represent financial assistance:

(a)   Distributions by lawfully paid dividend or in the course of winding up.

    (b)   Allotment of bonus shares.

    (c)   Reduction of capital confirmed by court order.

    (d)   The redemption or purchase of own shares.

    (e)   A scheme of arrangement between the company and members or creditors under section 206 of the 1948 Act or an arrangement under sections 287 or 306 of the 1948 Act.

Private companies

25   A private company may give financial assistance for the purchase of its own shares or, if its holding company and any intermediate holding companies are all private companies, its holding company's shares, provided that: 1981 s 43(1), (3)

    (a)   the net assets of the company are not thereby reduced, or the reduction is provided out of distributable profits;   1981 s 43(2)

    (b)   before the financial assistance is given the directors of the company make a statutory declaration that immediately after the financial assistance has been given there will be no grounds on which the company would be found unable to pay its debts and the company will be able to pay its debts as they fall due during the next 12 months. Where the shares to be acquired are those of the holding company the directors of that company and of any intermediate holding company must also make an equivalent statutory declaration;   1981 s 43(6)–(7)

    (c)   the statutory declaration has annexed to it a report by the auditors of the company to the directors stating that they have enquired into the company's state of affairs and that they are not aware of anything to indicate that the directors' opinion is unreasonable in all the circumstances;   1981 s 43(8)

    (d)   the giving of financial assistance is approved by special resolution in general meeting, passed within one week of the statutory declaration. No special resolution is required where the company is a wholly owned subsidiary. Where the shares to be acquired are those of the holding company, approval by that company (and any partly owned intermediate holding company) by special resolution in general meeting is also required. The statutory declaration and auditors' report thereon must be available for inspection at the meeting at which the resolution is passed;   1981 s 43(4)–(5) 1981 s 44(1) 1981 s 44(4)

    (e)   the financial assistance is not given before four weeks after the special resolution (if required) is passed or after eight weeks from the date of the statutory declaration.   1981 s 43(9)

26   The statutory declaration, the auditors' report thereon, and a copy of the   1981 s 44(5) special resolution passed (if applicable) must be delivered to the registrar within 15 days after the passing of the resolution or, if no resolution is necessary, after the making of the statutory declaration.

27   The holders of not less than 10 per cent of the company's issued shares or   1981 s 44(2) any class thereof who had either not consented to, or not voted in favour of, the special resolution may apply to the court for the resolution to be cancelled. The court may make an order on such terms as it thinks fit either confirming or cancelling the resolution.

Share Premiums

28   Where a company issues shares at a premium (whether for cash or otherwise)   1948 s 56 the amount or value of the premium must be transferred to a share premium account, except as set out below.

29   The premium on the issue of shares on or after 4 February 1981 does not have to be transferred to a share premium account where:

     (a)   a company secures at least a 90 per cent equity holding in another   1981 s 37 company in any arrangement which provides for the allotment of equity shares by the issuing company to the shareholders in the other company. If the arrangement also provides for the allotment of any shares by the company in return for non-equity shares acquired from the other company or for the cancellation of any such shares not held by the issuing company the relief extends to those shares;

     (b)   in a group reconstruction, a wholly owned subsidiary allots shares to its   1981 s 38 holding company or another wholly owned subsidiary in consideration for the transfer to it of shares in another subsidiary (whether wholly owned or not). However in this case a 'minimum premium value', which is the lesser of the cost or book value of the shares to the transferring company over the nominal value of the shares issued must be transferred to the share premium account of the issuing company.

30   However, care is required in interpreting the Act — in particular as to what constitutes an 'arrangement providing for the allotment of equity shares'. Whilst it would seem that relief is available to the extent that shares are issued even where there is a cash or loan stock element or alternative, this and the effect of market purchases will need to be reviewed with legal advisers.

31   The Act does not attempt to prescribe the appropriate accounting treatment for business combinations and it is therefore open to the Accounting Standards Committee to prepare an accounting standard on this subject in the future.

32   For shares issued at a premium before 4 February 1981, there is retrospective relief from the requirements of section 56 of the 1948 Act. This is given in respect of share for share exchanges which resulted in a subsidiary being acquired, but only if the transaction was accounted for at that time as a merger.   1981 s 39

33   The Secretary of State is empowered to give further relief from the requirements of the 1948 Act or to restrict or modify the relief given in the 1981 Act.   1981 s 41

34   It is understood that this power of the Secretary of State is to allow for any changes necessary when the EEC Seventh Directive (Group Accounts) is enacted in Great Britain.

Distributions of Profits and Assets

Profits available for distribution

35   No company may make a distribution except out of profits available for the purpose. The definition of profits available for distribution is more restrictive for a public company than for a private company.   1980 s 39(1)
Author

Meaning of distribution

36   A distribution means any distribution of the company's assets to its members other than by way of: 1980 s 45(2)
(amended by 1981 3 sch 48)

(a)   an issue of shares as fully or partly paid bonus shares; or

(b)   the redemption or purchase of any of the company's own shares out of capital (including the proceeds of a fresh issue) or out of unrealised profits; or

(c)   a reduction of share capital; or

(d)   a distribution on winding up.

Private companies

37   For private companies, profits available for distribution are a company's accumulated realised profits, so far as not previously utilised by distribution or capitalisation, less its accumulated realised losses so far as not previously written off in a reduction or reorganisation of capital.   1980 s 39(2)

38   Taking account of the prudence concept embodied in SSAP 2, the amount of profits legally distributable should, *prima facie*, be the accumulated balance of retained profits shown in the accounts. However, this balance may be

subject to adjustment in determining the amount of profits legally distributable in the circumstances described below.

Public companies

39   A public company is bound by the rules for private companies but in addition can make a distribution only if at that time its net assets after making the distribution are at least equal to the aggregate of its called up share capital and undistributable reserves (as defined below). The effect of this is that a public company must deduct net unrealised losses (i.e. unrealised losses less unrealised profits) from net realised profits (i.e. realised profits less realised losses) before making a distribution.

1980 s 40(1)

Author

40   Undistributable reserves for this purpose are:

1980 s 40(2)

(a)   the share premium account;

(b)   the capital redemption reserve;

(c)   the excess of accumulated unrealised profits (where not previously capitalised, which means all forms of capitalisation except transfers to a capital redemption reserve) over accumulated unrealised losses (where not previously written off in a reduction or reorganisation of capital);

(d)   any other reserve which is not distributable (e.g. because of provisions in the memorandum or Articles).

Realised profits and losses

41   The 1981 Act states that only profits 'realised' at the balance sheet date can be included in the profit and loss account. 'Realised profits' are stated to be profits determined in accordance with accounting principles generally accepted. Thus profits included in the accounts in accordance with SSAPs are realised profits.

1981 1 sch 12, 90

Author

42   The recognition of profit only when realised, either in the form of cash or other assets the ultimate cash realisation of which can be assessed with reasonable certainty, is embodied in the prudence concept in SSAP 2.

43   For the purpose of calculating realised profits, where a company makes a distribution of, or the distribution includes, any non-cash asset and any part of the book value of that asset represents an unrealised profit, the act of distribution will be regarded as an act of realisation and that profit must be treated as a realised profit.

1980 s 43A
(introduced by 1981 s 85)

44   The meaning of 'realised losses' is not explained in the Act. However, it is stated that any provision, except for a provision in respect of any diminution

1980 s 39(4)
(amended by 1981 3 sch 4

in value of a fixed asset appearing on a revaluation of all the fixed assets or of all the fixed assets other than goodwill (see below), must be treated as a realised loss. A provision is defined in schedule 1 to the 1981 Act and comprises provisions for depreciation and diminution in value of assets and provisions for liabilities or losses.

1981 1 sch 87–88

45   Development costs, even if carried forward as an asset, must be treated as a realised loss. This does not apply if:

1980 s 42A
(introduced by 1981 s 84)

(a)   there are special circumstances justifying the directors in deciding that the amount should not be treated as a realised loss (see Chapter 5); and

(b)   the note to the accounts giving reasons for including development costs as an asset (required by paragraph 20 of schedule 1 to the 1981 Act) states that the asset is not to be treated as a realised loss and explains the circumstances relied upon to justify the decision of the directors to that effect.

Revaluations of fixed assets
Revaluation reserve

46   The 1981 Act requires any profit or loss arising on the revaluation of an asset to be accounted for in a revaluation reserve, to be disclosed separately in the accounts. The amount of the revaluation reserve must be reduced by the directors if in their opinion any part of it is no longer necessary for the purpose of the company's accounting policies. However, such an amount may only be transferred to the profit and loss account if either:

(a)   the amount in question was previously charged to that account; or
(b)   it represents realised profit.

Deficits on revaluations of fixed assets

47   Where certain fixed assets or a class or classes of fixed assets are revalued it would seem that under section 39(4) of the 1980 Act individual deficits are provisions, and therefore realised losses (unless offsetting a previous unrealised surplus on the same asset) and individual surpluses would be unrealised profits. However, as noted above this is not the case when a revaluation of all the fixed assets (or all the fixed assets except goodwill) has taken place. In these circumstances individual deficits should be treated as unrealised in the same way as individual surpluses against which they can be set off. As noted above, a private company does not have to make good net unrealised losses before making a distribution, and it would therefore seem to be the intention of the Act to treat private companies more liberally than public companies. The above comments are, however, subject to the following two provisos:

Author

1980 s 39(4), (4A)
(introduced by 1981 3 sch 45)

Author

(a)   Where on a revaluation of all the fixed assets there are surpluses and deficits leading to a net deficit, the law as outlined above would appear to provide that such deficit is unrealised, whether or not charged in the profit and loss account, and on that basis (for a private company) would not restrict the ability to pay dividends. However, in the authors' view:

(i)   the net deficit should be charged in the profit and loss account (to the extent that it is not covered by revaluation surpluses previously recognised on any of the assets concerned); and

(ii)   it would be commercially imprudent to disregard the net deficit in determining dividend policy.

(b)   The view has been expressed that a provision for permanent diminution in the value of a fixed asset required by paragraph 19(2) of schedule 1 to the 1981 Act should be charged in the profit and loss account and treated as a realised loss even if it arises on a revaluation of all the fixed assets. While the justification for this interpretation is not immediately obvious from the words of the Act, such treatment might be regarded as desirable on the grounds of accounting prudence.

48   A revaluation of all the fixed assets is deemed to have taken place in this context if the directors give consideration to the value of all fixed assets not actually revalued provided: | 1980 s 39(4A), (7A) (introduced by 1981 3 sch 45, 47)

(a)   they are satisfied that the aggregate value of those fixed assets is not less than their aggregate book value in the accounts; and

(b)   the relevant accounts refer to the directors' valuation in the notes.

49   This provision that the directors may consider the value of all of those fixed assets which are not included in the accounts at a valuation is significant. Individual valuation deficits recognised in the accounts will be treated as unrealised in these circumstances. For private companies this will ensure that the amount of distributable profits is not thereby reduced and for public companies that distributable profits will only be reduced if unrealised losses exceed unrealised profits. Thus, where the inclusion of certain fixed assets in the accounts at a valuation is proposed it would seem advantageous for the directors to consider the value of all fixed assets and make the necessary disclosure.

Depreciation on revalued fixed assets

50   Under the 1980 Act, where a fixed asset is revalued, written up in the balance sheet and subsequently depreciated, the depreciation charge relating to the revaluation surplus element will not be taken to reduce distributable profits. This may require companies to keep memorandum records of the accumulated depreciation on the revaluation element. However, many

1980 s 39(5)

Author

companies would regard it as imprudent to distribute profits without deducting this additional depreciation.

Uncertainty as to profits available

51   Where there is no record of the original cost of an asset, the earliest record of 'value' can be assumed to be 'cost' and the calculation of the surplus may be based on that figure.

1980 s 39(6)

52   Where directors, after making all reasonable enquiries, are unable to determine whether a particular profit or loss made before the day this section becomes operative was realised or not they may treat the profit as realised and the loss as unrealised.

1980 s 39(7)

Current cost accounts

53   Where a company presents current cost accounts as its main or only accounts it is not wholly clear whether the amount of legally distributable profits is affected. The depreciation adjustment will not affect the amount of distributable profits by virtue of section 39(5) of the 1980 Act (see above). It could also be argued that the other current cost adjustments do not affect the amount of distributable profits because the guidance notes to SSAP 16 indicate that the cumulative net total of current cost adjustments, insofar as it has been passed through the profit and loss account, included in the current cost reserve is realised. On the other hand the fact that these other adjustments are charged in the profit and loss account might imply that the amount of distributable profit is affected. Directors will need to consider this matter in deciding whether to prepare their main accounts on a current cost basis, although many would in any event regard it as imprudent to distribute part of the current cost reserve.

Paying up issued shares

54   An unrealised profit must not be applied in paying up debentures or unpaid amounts on its issued shares.

1980 s 39(3)

Relevant accounts

55   In order to calculate whether a company can make a distribution, the 'relevant accounts' must be referred to. These are:

1980 s 43(1)–(3)
(amended by 1981 3 sch 47)

(a)   the latest accounts laid before a general meeting; or

(b)   if basing the calculation only on (a) above would lead to a contravention of the Act, interim accounts 'to enable reasonable judgment to be made as to the amounts of the relevant items'; or

(c)   during a company's first accounting period, such initial accounts as are necessary.

56   Where the accounts used are the latest annual accounts, they must have been properly prepared (i.e. to give a true and fair view) or have been so prepared subject only to matters which are not material to the question of whether the distribution can be made, and must have been audited. If the audit report was qualified, the auditor must have stated in writing (either at the time or subsequently) whether the subject of the qualification is material for the purposes of determining whether the distribution proposed or to be proposed would contravene the Act. A copy of such a statement must have been laid before the company in general meeting.

1980 s 43(3)
(amended by
1981 3 sch 47)

57   The interim accounts referred to above must for a public company also be 'properly prepared' or have been so prepared, subject only to matters which are not material to the question of whether the distribution can be made. They must be in the English language and a copy should be delivered to the registrar. They do not have to be audited.

1980 s 43(5)

58   The initial accounts of a public company must also have been 'properly prepared' or have been so prepared subject only to matters which are not material to the question of whether the distribution can be made, and the same rules apply regarding the audit report as described above. The accounts must also be translated into English if necessary and be delivered to the registrar.

1980 s 43(6)

Memorandum and Articles

59   Where a company's memorandum or articles contain distribution restrictions more rigorous than those in this Act, such further restrictions still stand.

1980 s 45(5)

Investment companies

60   There are different restrictions on investment companies. These are set out in section 41 of the Companies Act 1980.

1980 s 41

Insurance companies

61   Insurance companies are allowed to treat as a realised profit (or conversely any deficit as a realised loss) any amount properly transferred to the profit and loss account from a surplus in the fund maintained by it in respect of long term business. 'Surplus' means an excess of assets representing the fund over the long term liabilities, as shown by an actuarial investigation as defined by section 14 of the Insurance Companies Act 1974, and a 'deficit' means the opposite.

1980 s 42

Application

62   The provisions relating to the legality of distributions apply to a public company originally incorporated as such from the date of incorporation and in the case of other companies from the earlier of:

    1980 s 45(6)

(a)   registration or reregistration of a company under the Act; or

(b)   the end of the transitional period (18 months from the appointed day, i.e. 22 June 1982).

Appendix 1

Balance Sheet and Profit and Loss Account Formats

This appendix reproduces the balance sheet and profit and loss account formats set out in the first schedule to the Companies Act 1981. The rules relating to the selection and modification of these formats are explained in Chapter 3.

Balance Sheet Format 1

A **Called up share capital not paid**

B **Fixed assets**

   I   Intangible assets
      1 Development costs
      2 Concessions, patents, licences, trade marks and similar rights and assets
      3 Goodwill
      4 Payments on account

  II Tangible assets
      1 Land and buildings
      2 Plant and machinery
      3 Fixtures, fittings, tools and equipment
      4 Payments on account and assets in course of construction

 III Investments
      1 Shares in group companies
      2 Loans to group companies
      3 Shares in related companies
      4 Loans to related companies
      5 Other investments other than loans
      6 Other loans
      7 Own shares

C   **Current assets**

I   Stocks
    1   Raw materials and consumables
    2   Work in progress
    3   Finished goods and goods for resale
    4   Payments on account

II   Debtors
    1   Trade debtors
    2   Amounts owed by group companies
    3   Amounts owed by related companies
    4   Other debtors
    5   Called up share capital not paid
    6   Prepayments and accrued income

III   Investments
    1   Shares in group companies
    2   Own shares
    3   Other investments

IV   Cash at bank and in hand

D   **Prepayments and accrued income**

E   **Creditors: amounts falling due within one year**
    1   Debenture loans
    2   Bank loans and overdrafts
    3   Payments received on account
    4   Trade creditors
    5   Bills of exchange payable
    6   Amounts owed to group companies
    7   Amounts owed to related companies
    8   Other creditors including taxation and social security
    9   Accruals and deferred income

F   **Net current assets (liabilities)**

G   **Total assets less current liabilities**

H   **Creditors: amounts falling due after more than one year**
  1 Debenture loans
  2 Bank loans and overdrafts
  3 Payments received on account
  4 Trade creditors
  5 Bills of exchange payable
  6 Amounts owed to group companies
  7 Amounts owed to related companies
  8 Other creditors including taxation and social security
  9 Accruals and deferred income

I   **Provisions for liabilities and charges**
  1 Pensions and similar obligations
  2 Taxation, including deferred taxation
  3 Other provisions

J   **Accruals and deferred income**

K   **Capital and reserves**

  I   Called up share capital

  II   Share premium account

  III   Revaluation reserve

  IV   Other reserves
    1 Capital redemption reserve
    2 Reserve for own shares
    3 Reserves provided for by the Articles of Association
    4 Other reserves

  V   Profit and loss account

Balance Sheet Format 2

ASSETS

A   **Called up share capital not paid**

B   **Fixed assets**

    I   Intangible assets
        1 Development costs
        2 Concessions, patents, licences, trade marks and similar rights and assets
        3 Goodwill
        4 Payments on account

    II   Tangible assets
        1 Land and buildings
        2 Plant and machinery
        3 Fixtures, fittings, tools and equipment
        4 Payments on account and assets in course of construction

    III Investments
        1 Shares in group companies
        2 Loans to group companies
        3 Shares in related companies
        4 Loans to related companies
        5 Other investments other than loans
        6 Other loans
        7 Own shares

C   **Current assets**

    I   Stocks
        1 Raw materials and consumables
        2 Work in progress
        3 Finished goods and goods for resale
        4 Payments on account

    II   Debtors
        1 Trade debtors
        2 Amounts owed by group companies
        3 Amounts owed by related companies
        4 Other debtors
        5 Called up share capital not paid
        6 Prepayments and accrued income

    III   Investments
         1   Shares in group companies
         2   Own shares
         3   Other investments

    IV   Cash at bank and in hand

D   **Prepayments and accrued income**

LIABILITIES

A   **Capital and reserves**

    I   Called up share capital

    II   Share premium account

    III   Revaluation reserve

    IV   Other reserves
         1   Capital redemption reserve
         2   Reserve for own shares
         3   Reserves provided for by the Articles of Association
         4   Other reserves

    V   Profit and loss account

B   **Provisions for liabilities and charges**
         1   Pensions and similar obligations
         2   Taxation including deferred taxation
         3   Other provisions

C   **Creditors**
         1   Debenture loans
         2   Bank loans and overdrafts
         3   Payments received on account
         4   Trade creditors
         5   Bills of exchange payable
         6   Amounts owed to group companies
         7   Amounts owed to related companies
         8   Other creditors including taxation and social security
         9   Accruals and deferred income

D   **Accruals and deferred income**

Profit and Loss Account Format 1

1   Turnover
2   Cost of sales
3   Gross profit or loss
4   Distribution costs
5   Administrative expenses
6   Other operating income
7   Income from shares in group companies
8   Income from shares in related companies
9   Income from other fixed asset investments
10 Other interest receivable and similar income
11 Amounts written off investments
12 Interest payable and similar charges
13 Tax on profit or loss on ordinary activities
14 Profit or loss on ordinary activities after taxation
15 Extraordinary income
16 Extraordinary charges
17 Extraordinary profit or loss
18 Tax on extraordinary profit or loss
19 Other taxes not shown under the above items
20 Profit or loss for the financial year

Profit and Loss Account Format 2

1   Turnover
2   Change in stocks of finished goods and in work in progress
3   Own work capitalised
4   Other operating income
5   (a)   Raw materials and consumables
   (b)   Other external charges
6   Staff costs:
   (a)   Wages and salaries
   (b)   Social security costs
   (c)   Other pension costs
7   (a)   Depreciation and other amounts written off tangible and intangible fixed assets
   (b)   Exceptional amounts written off current assets
8   Other operating charges
9   Income from shares in group companies
10 Income from shares in related companies
11 Income from other fixed asset investments
12 Other interest receivable and similar income
13 Amounts written off investments
14 Interest payable and similar charges
15 Tax on profit or loss on ordinary activities
16 Profit or loss on ordinary activities after taxation
17 Extraordinary income
18 Extraordinary charges
19 Extraordinary profit or loss
20 Tax on extraordinary profit or loss
21 Other taxes not shown under the above items
22 Profit or loss for the financial year

Profit and Loss Account Format 3

A   **Charges**
1   Cost of sales
2   Distribution costs
3   Administrative expenses
4   Amounts written off investments
5   Interest payable and similar charges
6   Tax on profit or loss on ordinary activities
7   Profit or loss on ordinary activities after taxation
8   Extraordinary charges
9   Tax on extraordinary profit or loss
10 Other taxes not shown under the above items
11 Profit or loss for the financial year

B   **Income**
1   Turnover
2   Other operating income
3   Income from shares in group companies
4   Income from shares in related companies
5   Income from other fixed asset investments
6   Other interest receivable and similar income
7   Profit or loss on ordinary activities after taxation
8   Extraordinary income
9   Profit or loss for the financial year

Profit and Loss Account Format 4

A   **Charges**
1. Reduction in stocks of finished goods and in work in progress
2. (a) Raw materials and consumables
   (b) Other external charges
3. Staff costs:
   (a) Wages and salaries
   (b) Social security costs
   (c) Other pension costs
4. (a) Depreciation and other amounts written off tangible and intangible fixed assets
   (b) Exceptional amounts written off current assets
5. Other operating charges
6. Amounts written off investments
7. Interest payable and similar charges
8. Tax on profit or loss on ordinary activities
9. Profit or loss on ordinary activities after taxation
10. Extraordinary charges
11. Tax on extraordinary profit or loss
12. Other taxes not shown under the above items
13. Profit or loss for the financial year

B   **Income**
1. Turnover
2. Increase in stocks of finished goods and in work in progress
3. Own work capitalised
4. Other operating income
5. Income from shares in group companies
6. Income from shares in related companies
7. Income from other fixed asset investments
8. Other interest receivable and similar income
9. Profit or loss on ordinary activities after taxation
10. Extraordinary income
11. Profit or loss for the financial year

Appendix 2 — White plc

White plc is designed to provide an example of the accounts of a listed group that embody substantially all the more common statutory and other requirements dealt with in this book.

In many respects the methods of disclosure, and particularly the wording of notes, represent the authors' suggestion rather than mandatory format; in practice, of course, annual accounts are drafted in the particular circumstances of individual companies and groups and will show significant variations from the authors' example.

The White plc accounts are drawn up for the year to 31 March 1983 because it is unlikely that the requirements of the Companies Act 1981 will become applicable before 1982/83.

WHITE PLC

Report of the Directors for the Year Ended 31 March 1983

1   The directors present herewith the audited accounts for the year ended 31 March 1983.

Review of activities and post balance sheet events

2   The consolidated profit and loss account for the year is set out on page 128.

The main activities of the group are unchanged since last year, and are principally the manufacture of:

(a) solid state electronics for the TV, radio and medical equipment industries;
(b) moulded plastics for packing materials;
(c) prefabricated building sections;
(d) domestic appliances, principally washing machines and deep-freezers.

Both the level of business and the year end financial position were satisfactory, and the directors expect that the present level of activity will be sustained for the foreseeable future.

On 1 April 1982 the company acquired, for cash, the whole of the issued share capital of Brown plc, manufacturers of building materials. Details of the assets acquired and consideration paid are set out at the foot of the statement of source and application of funds on page 135. In the current year, Brown plc had a turnover of £3 million, and made a profit after taxation of £100,000.

In line with the group's policy of long term expansion and diversification through the acquisition of soundly based companies, the board made an offer on 29 May 1983 for the whole of the issued share capital of Crimson plc. This offer is conditional upon the approval of the members of White plc, and is to be voted upon at the annual general meeting.

Crimson plc supplies high technology equipment to the offshore oil and gas industries, and in the year to 31 December 1982 made an attributable profit of £1 million on a turnover of £6 million. The offer is for £5 million which will, if accepted, be financed by a long term secured loan.

Dividends

3   The directors have declared or now recommend the following dividends in respect of the year ended 31 March 1983:

	£	£
Preference dividends already paid		67,200
Ordinary dividends:		
Interim of 0.75p per share paid on 19 October 1982	290,580	
Proposed final of 1.75p per share payable on 20 August 1983	678,020	
		968,600
		£1,035,800

The balance of the profit for the year will be carried to revenue reserve.

Directors

4   The directors of the company at 31 March 1983, all of whom have been directors for the whole of the year ended on that date, were:

Mr C Jones (Chairman)
Mr H Smith (Managing Director)
Mr F Walsh*
Mr S Davies
Mr C Visser (Dutch)

Mr D Scott, who was a director at 1 April 1982, resigned on 30 September 1982 on his retirement from the business.

In accordance with the Articles of Association, Mr F Walsh retires by rotation and, being eligible, offers himself for reelection.

*Mr Walsh has a service contract with the company which expires on 31 July 1984.

Changes in fixed assets

5   The movements in fixed assets during the year are set out in notes 14 to 16 to the accounts. An extensive programme of plant replacement has been undertaken during the year. Land and buildings in Derby, no longer required, have been sold.

Market value of interests in land

6   In the opinion of the directors, the current open market value on an existing use basis of the freehold and leasehold land and buildings exceeded the amount of £6,346,000 at which they are included in the balance sheet at 31 March 1983 by approximately £5 million.

Realisation at the balance sheet date at the estimated value of £11.5 million would have resulted in a tax liability of approximately £1.5 million, together with a further £850,000 of rolled over capital gains which would then have crystallised.

Directors' interests in shares of the company

7   The interests of the directors of the company at 31 March 1983 in shares of the company, according to the register required to be kept by section 29 of the Companies Act 1967, were as follows:

Ordinary shares of 25p each

| | **31 March 1983** | | **1 April 1982** | |
	Number	*Nominal value £*	*Number*	*Nominal value £*
Mr C Jones	66,000†	16,500	46,000†	11,500
Mr H Smith	95,700††	23,925	87,000††	21,750
Mr F Walsh	—	—	—	—
Mr S Davies	3,000	750	3,000	750
Mr C Visser	—	—	—	—
	164,700	£41,175	136,000	£34,000

†Both these totals include 20,000 shares in which Mr Jones and his wife are interested under a family settlement.

††In addition, Mr Smith has an interest in 10,000 ordinary shares of 25p each by virtue of his option — see paragraph 8 below.

No directors were interested at any time during the year in any of the preference shares of the company, nor in the share capital of the company's subsidiaries, nor in any of the loan stock of the company or its subsidiaries.

There has been no change in the interests set out above between 31 March 1983 and 30 May 1983 (a date within one month of the notice of the annual general meeting).

Option granted to a director

8   By an agreement dated 2 February 1982 between Mr Smith and the company, Mr Smith was granted an option to subscribe for up to 10,000 ordinary shares of 25p each in the company. This option is exercisable at any time before 1 December 1986 at a price of 55p per share; no part of it had been exercised at 31 March 1983.

Directors' interests in contracts

9   None of the directors had a material interest in any contract of significance to which the company, or a subsidiary, was a party during the financial year.

Group research and development activities

10   The group is heavily committed to research and development activities so as to secure its position as market leader in sectors of the electrical components and domestic appliances markets. In addition to the expenditure set out in note 14 to the accounts, £147,000 of costs attributable to pure and applied research have been written off in the year.

Substantial shareholdings

11   With the exception of the interest of Mega-White plc (see note 32 on page 162), the directors have not been advised of any individual interest, or group of interests held by persons acting together, which at 19 June 1983 exceeded 5 per cent of the company's issued share capital.

Political and charitable contributions

12   Contributions made by the group during the year for political and charitable purposes were:

	£
For political purposes — the Hotair Party	250
For charitable purposes	4,320
	£4,570

Disabled persons

13   The group's policy is to recruit disabled workers for those vacancies that they are able to fill. All necessary assistance with initial training courses is given. Once employed, a career plan is developed so as to ensure suitable opportunities for each disabled person.

Close company provisions

14   As far as the directors are aware, the close company provisions of the Income and Corporation Taxes Act 1970, as amended, do not apply to the company. There has been no change in this respect since the end of the financial year.

Auditors

15   A resolution to reappoint the auditors, Moorgate Place & Co, will be proposed at the annual general meeting.

BY ORDER OF THE BOARD

19 June 1983

A E MACFARLANE
Secretary

Report of the Auditors to the Members of White plc

We have audited the accounts set out on pages 128 to 172 in accordance with approved Auditing Standards. The accounts on pages 128 to 162 have been prepared under the historical cost convention modified by the revaluation of certain fixed assets, and the supplementary accounts on pages 163 to 172 have been prepared under the current cost convention as described in Statement of Standard Accounting Practice No 16.

In our opinion the accounts on pages 128 to 172 give, under the respective conventions described above, a true and fair view of the state of affairs of the company and the group at 31 March 1983 and of the profit and source and application of funds of the group for the year then ended and comply with the Companies Acts 1948 to 1981.

Moorgate Place & Co

London, 19 June 1983

Chartered Accountants

WHITE PLC
and its subsidiary companies
**Consolidated Profit and Loss Account for
the year ended 31 March 1983**

	Notes	1983 £'000	1982 £'000
Turnover	2	65,720	53,824
Cost of sales		45,489	37,450
Gross profit		20,231	16,374
Net operating expenses	3	17,037	13,380
Operating profit	4	3,194	2,994
Share of profits less losses of related companies	7	320	160
Income from other fixed asset investments	7	274	94
		594	254
Interest payable and similar charges	8	734	639
Profit before taxation		3,054	2,609
Tax on profit on ordinary activities	9	1,449	1,298
Profit on ordinary activities after taxation		1,605	1,311
Profit attributable to minority interests		411	162
Profit after tax, and before extraordinary income		1,194	1,149
Extraordinary income, less minority interests and tax	10	284	—
Profit for the financial year attributable to the shareholders of White plc	11	1,478	1,149
Dividends paid and proposed	12	1,036	939
Retained profit for the year	27	442	210
Earnings per ordinary share	13	2.91p	2.79p

The notes on pages 136 to 162 form part of these accounts.
Auditors' report page 127.

WHITE PLC
and its subsidiary companies
**Consolidated Profit and Loss Account for
the year ended 31 March 1983 — continued**

Statement of Consolidated Retained Profits

	Notes	1983 £'000	1982 £'000
Retained profits at 1 April 1982			
As previously reported		10,651	10,185
Restatement arising from change in accounting policy	14(a)	(279)	(166)
As restated		10,372	10,019
Exchange difference arising from retranslation of opening net investment in foreign subsidiaries		159	135
		10,531	10,154
Exchange difference arising from the translation of subsidiary companies' results at average rather than closing date		13	8
Retained profit for the year		442	210
		455	218
Retained profits at 31 March 1983		10,986	10,372

The notes on pages 136 to 162 form part of these accounts.
Auditors' report page 127.

WHITE PLC
and its subsidiary companies
Consolidated Balance Sheet — 31 March 1983

	Notes	1983		1982	
		£'000	£'000	£'000	£'000
Fixed assets					
Intangible assets	14		1,138		1,205
Tangible assets	15		29,858		28,292
Investments:					
Shares in related companies	16	417		367	
Other investments other than loans	16	617		466	
			1,034		833
			32,030		30,330
Current assets					
Stocks	17	7,821		8,004	
Debtors	18	8,039		8,226	
Investments	19	166		247	
Cash at bank and in hand		561		336	
		16,587		16,813	
Creditors — amounts falling due within one year	20	8,056		9,325	
Net current assets			8,531		7,488
Total assets less current liabilities			40,561		37,818
Less: Non-current liabilities					
Creditors — amounts falling due after more than one year	21	7,475		5,780	
Provisions for liabilities and charges					
Pensions and similar obligations	22	151		103	
Taxation, including deferred taxation	23	509		686	
		660		789	
			8,135		6,569
			32,426		31,249

The notes on pages 136 to 162 form part of these accounts.
Auditors' report page 127.

WHITE PLC
and its subsidiary companies
Consolidated Balance Sheet — 31 March 1983 — continued

	Notes	1983		1982	
		£'000	£'000	£'000	£'000
Capital and reserves					
Called up share capital	24	10,886		10,886	
Share premium account		1,512		1,512	
Revaluation reserve	26	6,263		5,865	
Profit and loss account	27	10,986		10,372	
			29,647		28,635
Minority interests			2,779		2,614
			32,426		31,249

C JONES ⎫
H SMITH ⎭ Directors

The notes on pages 136 to 162 form part of these accounts.
Auditors' report page 127.

WHITE PLC

Balance Sheet — 31 March 1983

	Notes	1983 £'000	1983 £'000	1982 £'000	1982 £'000
Fixed assets					
Tangible assets	15		9,518		9,401
Investments:					
Shares in group companies	31	8,026		7,381	
Shares in related companies	16	182		182	
Other investments other than loans	16	216		143	
			8,424		7,706
			17,942		17,107
Current assets					
Stocks	17	3,269		3,586	
Debtors	18	4,384		4,418	
Investments	19	166		247	
Cash at bank and in hand		546		312	
		8,365		8,563	
Creditors — amounts falling due within one year	20	5,426		5,820	
Net current assets			2,939		2,743
Total assets less current liabilities			20,881		19,850
Less: Non-current liabilities					
Creditors — amounts falling due after more than one year	21	3,000		2,000	
Provisions for liabilities and charges					
Taxation, including deferred taxation	23	17		116	
			3,017		2,116
			17,864		17,734

The notes on pages 136 to 162 form part of these accounts.
Auditors' report page 127.

WHITE PLC

Balance Sheet — 31 March 1983 — continued

	Notes	1983 £'000	1983 £'000	1982 £'000	1982 £'000
Capital and reserves					
Called up share capital	24		10,886		10,886
Share premium account			1,512		1,512
Profit and loss account	27		5,466		5,336
			17,864		17,734

These accounts were approved by the board on 19 June 1983.

C JONES ⎫
H SMITH ⎭ Directors

The notes on pages 136 to 162 form part of these accounts.
Auditors' report page 127.

WHITE PLC
and its subsidiary companies
Consolidated Statement of Source and Application
of Funds for the year ended 31 March 1983

	1983 £'000	1983 £'000	1982 £'000	1982 £'000
Source of funds				
Profit before taxation		3,054		2,609
Adjustments for items not involving the movement of funds:				
Income from shares in related companies not represented by dividends received	(210)		(103)	
Depreciation of tangible fixed assets	4,075		3,101	
Amortisation of intangible fixed assets	320		378	
Pension provision	48		49	
Loss on sale of plant and fittings	85		98	
		4,318		3,523
Total from operations		7,372		6,132
Funds from other sources				
Sale proceeds of fixed assets	1,895		549	
Issue of $16\frac{1}{2}\%$ unsecured loan stock	1,000		—	
Secured loans	995		147	
Regional development grants received	790		527	
		4,680		1,223
Total sources of funds		12,052		7,355
Application of funds				
Dividends paid:				
To shareholders of White plc	1,036		939	
To minority shareholders in subsidiaries	272		147	
Tax paid	1,180		1,136	
Purchase of fixed assets*	7,618		3,556	
Purchase of goodwill*	18		—	
Purchase of investments	151		107	
Deferred development expenditure	235		272	
Total applications of funds		(10,510)		(6,157)
Increase in working capital		1,542		1,198

*See page 135.   Auditors' report page 127.

WHITE PLC
and its subsidiary companies
Consolidated Statement of Source and Application
of Funds for the year ended 31 March 1983 — continued

	1983		1982	
	£'000	£'000	£'000	£'000
Increase in working capital				
(Decrease)/increase in stocks*	(183)		366	
(Decrease)/increase in debtors*	(187)		282	
Decrease in current creditors, excluding taxation, proposed dividends, overdrafts and debentures	1,815		123	
Exchange adjustments taken to reserves in respect of working capital	(131)		(71)	
		1,314		700
Movement in net liquid funds:				
Bank and cash balances	309		431	
Short term investments	(81)		67	
		228		498
Increase in working capital		1,542		1,198

*Summary of the effects of the acquisition of Brown plc.

	£'000
Net assets acquired:	
Fixed assets	1,072
Stocks and work in progress	120
Debtors	100
Creditors	(651)
	641
Goodwill	18
Cash paid	659

Auditors' report page 127.

WHITE PLC
and its subsidiary companies
Notes to the Accounts — 31 March 1983

1 **Principal accounting policies**

A summary of the more important group accounting policies is set out below. The policy in respect of goodwill has been changed from that adopted in the 1982 accounts.

(a) **Basis of consolidation**
The consolidated accounts include the company and all its subsidiaries. The results of subsidiaries acquired or disposed of during the year are included in the consolidated profit and loss account from the date of their acquisition or up to the date of their disposal. Intra group sales and profits are eliminated on consolidation and all sales and profit figures relate to external transactions only.

The excess of the purchase price over the value of the net assets of subsidiary companies at the date of acquisition is included in the consolidated balance sheet as goodwill arising on consolidation. The accounting treatment of such goodwill is explained in note 14(a) below.

(b) **Related companies**
The group's share of profits less losses of related companies is included in the consolidated profit and loss account, and the group's share of post acquisition retained profits and reserves is added to the cost of the investments in the consolidated balance sheet. These amounts are taken from the latest audited balance sheets of the companies concerned, which in all cases are made up to dates not more than three months prior to the end of the financial year of the group. Since the accounting policies of related companies do not necessarily conform in all respects with those of the group, adjustments are made on consolidation where the amounts involved are material to the group.

(c) **Fixed assets**
Interests in land and buildings are stated at current replacement cost, and are subject to annual revaluations. The basis of valuation is explained in note H(b) to the current cost accounts. The cost of other fixed assets is their purchase cost, together with any incidental expenses of acquisition. Regional development grants received or receivable on qualifying expenditure are applied in reduction of the cost of acquisition of the fixed assets to which the grants relate. As a result, grants are effectively credited to revenue over the expected useful lives of the related assets.

Depreciation is calculated so as to write off the cost of fixed assets, including goodwill, on a straight line basis over the expected useful economic lives of the assets concerned. The principal annual rates used for this purpose which, except for goodwill, are consistent with those of last year, are:

%

Freehold buildings   2
Precision plant   25

WHITE PLC
and its subsidiary companies
Notes to the Accounts — **31 March 1983** — **continued**

	%
Other plant	10
Motor vehicles	25
Furniture, fixtures and fittings	15
Purchased goodwill	20
Goodwill arising upon consolidation	3–5

Leasehold land and buildings are amortised over 50 years or the period of the lease, whichever is the less. Freehold land is not depreciated.

(d) Stocks and work in progress
Stocks and work in progress are stated at the lower of cost and net realisable value. In general, cost is determined on a first in first out basis and includes transport and handling costs; in the case of manufactured products cost includes all direct expenditure and production overheads based on the normal level of activity. Net realisable value is the price at which stocks can be sold in the normal course of business after allowing for the costs of realisation and, where appropriate, the cost of conversion from their existing state to a finished condition. Provision is made where necessary for obsolescent, slow moving and defective stocks.

(e) Investment income
Income from investments, other than from related companies, is included, together with the related tax credit, in the consolidated profit and loss account of the accounting period in which it is received.

(f) Foreign currencies
Assets and liabilities expressed in foreign currencies are translated to sterling at rates of exchange ruling at the end of the financial year, and the results of foreign subsidiaries are translated at the average rate of exchange for the whole year. Differences on exchange arising from the retranslation of the opening net investment in subsidiary companies, and from the translation of the results of those companies at average rate, are taken to reserves. Those differences attributable to revaluation surpluses are taken to the revaluation reserve.

(g) Turnover
Turnover, which excludes value added tax, sales between group companies and trade discount, represents the invoiced value of goods and services supplied.

(h) Taxation
The charge for taxation is based on the profit for the year as adjusted for disallowable items, and for timing differences to the extent that they are unlikely to result in an actual tax liability in the foreseeable future. Timing differences arise from the recognition for tax purposes of certain items of income and expenses in a different accounting period from that in which they are recognised in the accounts. The tax effect of other timing differences as reduced by the tax benefit of any accumulated losses is treated as a deferred tax liability.

(i) Development expenditure
Development expenditure relating to specific projects intended for commercial exploitation is carried

WHITE PLC
and its subsidiary companies
Notes to the Accounts — 31 March 1983 — continued

forward. Such expenditure is amortised over the periods expected to benefit from it commencing with the period in which related sales are first made. Expenditure on pure and applied research is written off as incurred.

(j) **Warranties for products**
Provision is made for the estimated liability on all products still under warranty, including claims already received.

(k) **Pension scheme arrangements**
The pension schemes of the group are externally funded. Payments made to the funds and charged annually in these accounts comprise current service contributions and back service contributions which are estimates based on actuarial advice. The funds are actuarially valued every three years.

2   **Turnover**

The contributions of the various activities of the group to turnover and profit before taxation are set out below:

	1983		1982	
	Turnover	Profit before tax	Turnover	Profit before tax
	£ million	£ million	£ million	£ million
Principal activities				
Electrical components	17.4	1.2	14.5	1.0
Moulded plastics	9.9	0.3	9.7	0.7
Building materials	21.4	0.6	17.8	0.8
Domestic appliances	17.0	1.0	11.8	0.1
	65.7	3.1	53.8	2.6
Geographical analysis				
United Kingdom	42.7		33.4	
Rest of Europe	10.1		9.8	
North America	8.3		6.8	
Africa	4.6		3.8	
	65.7		53.8	

WHITE PLC
and its subsidiary companies
Notes to the Accounts — 31 March 1983 — continued

3   **Net operating expenses**

Net operating expenses are made up as follows:

	1983 £'000	1982 £'000
Distribution costs	6,129	5,493
Administrative expenses	11,144	8,085
	17,273	13,578
Less: Other operating income — royalties	(236)	(198)
Net operating expenses	17,037	13,380

4   **Operating profit**

Operating profit is stated after charging:

	1983 £'000	1982 £'000
Auditors' remuneration for the group	25	22
Hire of plant and machinery	288	252
Depreciation of tangible fixed assets	4,075	3,101
Amortisation of intangible fixed assets	320	378
Directors' emoluments (see note 5) including pension contributions	136	114
Provision against other fixed asset investments (see note 16(b))	—	6

5   **Directors' emoluments**

Emoluments of directors of White plc (including pension contributions):

	1983 £	1982 £
As directors	2,150	2,150
For management services	130,253	97,775
	132,403	99,925
Pension paid to a former executive director of White plc	3,792	3,792
Compensation for loss of office paid to a former executive director of White plc	—	10,000
	£136,195	£113,717

WHITE PLC
and its subsidiary companies
Notes to the Accounts — 31 March 1983 — continued

Directors' emoluments, disclosed in accordance with sections 6 and 7 of the Companies Act 1967, and excluding pension contributions, are as follows:

	1983 £	1982 £
Emoluments of the Chairman	5,715	5,520
Emoluments of the highest paid director	38,500	34,000

Number of directors (excluding those above) whose emoluments were within the ranges:

	Number	Number
£10,001 to £15,000	1	—
£15,001 to £20,000	2	3
£25,001 to £30,000	1	—
Directors' emoluments waived:		
Number of directors concerned	—	1
Emoluments waived	—	£2,000

6   Employee information

(a) The average number of persons employed by the group including executive directors during the year is analysed below:

	1983	1982
By product group*		
Electrical components	1,783	1,677
Moulded plastics	223	257
Building materials	1,526	1,448
Domestic appliances	925	899
	4,457	4,281
By type of work*		
Production	3,343	3,425
Selling and distribution	668	514
Administration	446	342
	4,457	4,281

*Author's note: In practice only one of these analyses need be given.

WHITE PLC
and its subsidiary companies
Notes to the Accounts — 31 March 1983 — continued

	1983 £'000	1982 £'000
(b) Group employment costs — all employees including executive directors:		
Aggregate gross wages and salaries paid to the group's employees	20,131	18,392
Employers' national insurance contributions, or foreign equivalents	2,617	2,391
Employers' pension contributions under the group pension schemes	604	552
Total direct costs of employment	23,352	21,335

	Number	Number
(c) The number of employees of the holding company (excluding directors) whose emoluments were within the range:		
£20,001 to £25,000	1	—

7 **Income from fixed asset investments**

	1983 £'000	1982 £'000
Group's share in profits less losses before tax of related companies:		
Listed on a recognised stock exchange	197	62
Unlisted	123	98
	320	160
Income from fixed asset investments, other than related companies:		
Listed on a recognised stock exchange	146	37
Listed on other stock exchanges	53	29
	199	66
Unlisted	75	28
	274	94
Total income from fixed asset investments	594	254

Appendix 2

WHITE PLC
and its subsidiary companies
Notes to the Accounts — 31 March 1983 — continued

Income from shares in related companies:	1983 £'000	1982 £'000
Dividends received from listed companies	86	29
Dividends received from unlisted companies	24	28
	110	57

8 Interest payable and similar charges

	1983 £'000	1982 £'000
Interest payable on sums:		
Wholly repayable within five years	436	374
All others loans	298	265
Total interest payable and similar charges	734	639

9 Tax on profit on ordinary activities

The group

	1983 £'000	1982 £'000
United Kingdom corporation tax based on the profit for the year at 52 per cent (1982 — 52 per cent)	1,384	1,100
Transfer (from)/to deferred taxation	(177)	80
	1,207	1,180
Double tax relief	(25)	(17)
	1,182	1,163
Overseas taxation	82	46
Tax credit on United Kingdom dividends received	25	19
	1,289	1,228
Related companies		
Share of related companies' tax charge	160	70
	1,449	1,298

WHITE PLC
and its subsidiary companies
Notes to the Accounts — 31 March 1983 — continued

The charge for the year has been reduced in respect of stock relief and taxation deferred which is not expected to become payable in the foreseeable future. The amounts involved are:

	1983 £'000	1982 £'000
Stock relief	350	219
Accelerated capital allowances	380	264
	730	483

10 Extraordinary income

	1983 Attributable to the group £'000	Attributable to minority interests £'000	Total £'000	1982 £'000
Profit on disposal of properties	324	30	354	—
Less: Tax thereon	(40)	(4)	(44)	—
	284	26	310	—

11 Profit of White plc

£1,166,000 (1982 —£1,006,000) of the consolidated profit attributable to the shareholders of White plc has been dealt with in the accounts of that company. White plc has taken advantage of the legal dispensation allowing it not to publish a separate profit and loss account.

12 Dividends

	1983 £'000	1982 £'000
Preference — 5.6% paid	67	67
Ordinary:		
Interim of 0.75p per share paid (1982 — 0.5p per share)	291	194
Proposed final of 1.75p per share (1982 — 1.75p per share)	678	678
	969	872
	1,036	939

WHITE PLC
and its subsidiary companies
Notes to the Accounts — 31 March 1983 — continued

13   **Earnings per ordinary share**

Basic earnings per ordinary share of 25p each are calculated on the group profit, after taxation and minority interests and before the extraordinary item of £1,194,000 (1982 — £1,149,000) less preference dividends of £67,200 (1982 — £67,200), and on the 38,744,000 ordinary shares in issue during 1983 and 1982.

14   **Intangible fixed assets**

The company had no intangible fixed assets. Details of those relating to the group are as follows:

	Development expenditure £'000	Patents £'000	Purchased goodwill £'000	Goodwill on consolidation £'000	Total £'000
Cost					
At 1 April 1982	528	497	800	315	2,140
Expenditure	235	—	—	18	253
At 31 March 1983	763	497	800	333	2,393
Amortisation					
At 1 April 1982	305	351	200	79	935
Charge in year	178	28	100	14	320
At 31 March 1983	483	379	300	93	1,255
Net book value at 31 March 1983	280	118	500	240	1,138
Net book value at 31 March 1982	223	146	600	236	1,205

(a) The group's accounting policy in respect of purchased goodwill has been changed in order to comply with the requirements of the Companies Act 1981. The goodwill in question arose upon the purchase by Blue plc of an unincorporated business manufacturing electrical components. The manufacturing process is protected by a patent, which has five years left to run, and the goodwill will now be written off over that period. This approach was not adopted in the past because the board of Blue plc considered that research currently under way would have enabled that company to retain its position as market leader. This is still expected to be the case. The policy for accounting for goodwill arising upon consolidation has been changed so as to conform with that for purchased goodwill. Goodwill on consolidation is written off over periods varying between 20 and 30 years.

WHITE PLC
and its subsidiary companies
Notes to the Accounts — 31 March 1983 — continued

The effect of this change in accounting policy is shown below:

	Purchased goodwill £'000	Goodwill on consolidation £'000	Total £'000
Net book value of goodwill at 31 March 1982, as previously reported	800	315	1,115
Prior year adjustment	(200)	(79)	(279)
At 31 March 1982, as restated	600	236	836

(b) Development expenditure relates to specific projects undertaken by the electrical components and domestic appliances subsidiaries. The production of the electrical components concerned will commence next year, when the whole of the related development expenditure will be written off. The domestic appliances subsidiary has already started marketing the product which was the subject of earlier development expenditure. The production run is expected to last for three years, and the deferred expenditure is being written off over the same period.

WHITE PLC
and its subsidiary companies
Notes to the Accounts — 31 March 1983 — continued

15   Tangible fixed assets

The group

	Freehold land and buildings £'000	Leasehold land and buildings		Plant and machinery £'000	Fixtures and fittings £'000	Total £'000
		Long leases £'000	Short leases £'000			
Cost or valuation (see (a) below)						
At 1 April 1982	11,388	2,303	398	26,461	5,749	46,299
Exchange rate adjustments	315	—	—	247	54	616
New subsidiary	750	—	—	923	237	1,910
Expenditure	1,447	114	—	4,403	582	6,546
Revaluation	536	100	—	—	—	636
Regional development grants on capital expenditure	—	—	—	(790)	—	(790
Disposals	(2,075)	(467)	—	(3,355)	(192)	(6,089
At 31 March 1983	12,361	2,050	398	27,889	6,430	49,128
Depreciation						
At 1 April 1982	2,874	292	143	12,986	1,712	18,007
Exchange rate adjustments	233	—	40	222	57	552
New subsidiary	292	—	—	497	49	838
Charge for year	234	48	38	2,852	903	4,075
Disposals	(973)	(21)	—	(3,028)	(180)	(4,202
At 31 March 1983	2,660	319	221	13,529	2,541	19,270
Net book value at 31 March 1983	9,701	1,731	177	14,360	3,889	29,858
Net book value at 31 March 1982	8,514	2,011	255	13,475	4,037	28,292

WHITE PLC
and its subsidiary companies
Notes to the Accounts — 31 March 1983 — continued

(a) Interests in land and buildings are included at current cost. The historical cost and related depreciation of these properties are set out below:

	Freehold land and buildings £'000	Leasehold land and buildings	
		Long leases £'000	Short leases £'000
Cost			
At 1 April 1982	5,466	1,139	181
Exchange rate adjustments	117	—	—
New subsidiary	750	—	—
Expenditure	1,447	114	—
Disposals	(839)	(60)	—
At 31 March 1983	6,941	1,193	181
Depreciation			
At 1 April 1982	1,584	222	65
Exchange rate adjustments	98	—	—
New subsidiary	292	—	—
Charge for year	91	23	19
Disposals	(501)	(14)	—
At 31 March 1983	1,564	231	84
Historical cost net book value at 31 March 1983	5,377	962	97
Historical cost net book value at 31 March 1982	3,882	917	116

147

WHITE PLC
and its subsidiary companies
Notes to the Accounts — 31 March 1983 — continued

The potential tax liability, had these properties been sold at the balance sheet date for the amounts of their valuations, was:

	Freehold land and buildings £'000	Leasehold land and buildings	
		Long leases £'000	Short leases £'000
At 31 March 1983	1,297	232	23
At 31 March 1982	1,389	328	42

(b) Depreciation has not been charged on freehold land, which is stated at its revalued amount of £2,200,000 (1982 — £1,950,000).

(c) 'Fixtures and fittings' include tools and similar equipment.

The company

The fixed assets of White plc consist entirely of plant and machinery, as follows:

	Plant and machinery £'000
Cost at 1 April 1982	14,612
Additions	1,996
Cost at 31 March 1983	16,608
Depreciation at 1 April 1982	5,211
Charge for year	1,879
Depreciation at 31 March 1983	7,090
Net book value at 31 March 1983	9,518
Net book value at 31 March 1982	9,401

WHITE PLC
and its subsidiary companies
Notes to the Accounts — 31 March 1983 — continued

16　**Fixed asset investments**

Shares in related companies

	1983		1982	
	The company £'000	The group £'000	The company £'000	The group £'000
Unlisted shares at cost	182	182	182	182
Group's share of post acquisition retained profits and reserves	—	77	—	41
	182	259	182	223
Shares listed on The Stock Exchange, at cost	—	136	—	136
Group's share of post acquisition retained profits and reserves	—	22	—	8
	—	158	—	144
	182	417	182	367

The following information relates to shares in listed related companies:

Stock Exchange value at the balance sheet date	—	190	—	173
Tax that would have been payable had the investments been sold at the balance sheet date at their Stock Exchange values	—	16	—	11

WHITE PLC
and its subsidiary companies
Notes to the Accounts — 31 March 1983 — continued

Details of those companies in which the company held more than a 10 per cent interest (all of which are also related companies), are set out below:

Name of company	Description of shares held	Proportion of nominal value of ordinary shares held %	Accounting year end
Dee plc	Ordinary shares of 10p	32	31 March 1983
Gee Limited	Ordinary shares of £1	28	31 December 1982
Kay plc	Ordinary shares of 25p	37	31 December 1982

The shareholdings are held directly by White plc except in the case of Kay plc, where 5 per cent out of the total holding of 37 per cent is held by a wholly owned subsidiary. The principal country of operation of the above companies is the United Kingdom, and they are all registered in Scotland. Neither the company nor any subsidiary had any interest in the loan capital of these related companies.

Other fixed asset investments other than loans

	1983		1982	
	The company £'000	The group £'000	The company £'000	The group £'000
Shares listed on The Stock Exchange, at cost	119	403	92	299
Shares listed on other stock exchanges, at cost	31	72	13	69
Listed at cost	150	475	105	368
Unlisted shares, at cost	72	148	44	104
Less: Amounts written off	6	6	6	6
	66	142	38	98
Aggregate book value of listed and unlisted investments	216	617	143	466

WHITE PLC
and its subsidiary companies
Notes to the Accounts — 31 March 1983 — continued

	1983		1982	
	The company	The group	The company	The group
	£'000	£'000	£'000	£'000
Quoted value of investments listed on:				
The Stock Exchange	154	480	101	389
Other stock exchanges	39	86	15	82
	193	566	116	471
Contingent taxation liability:				
If the listed investments had been realised at the year end at the valuations shown above, there would have been taxation payable of	13	27	3	31

In no case did the company's interest in the shares in this subparagraph exceed 10 per cent.

17   **Stocks and work in progress**

The amounts attributable to the different categories are as follows:

	1983		1982	
	The company	The group	The company	The group
	£'000	£'000	£'000	£'000
Raw materials and consumables	1,027	1,636	1,001	1,820
Work in progress	1,266	3,876	1,634	3,979
Finished goods and goods for resale	976	2,309	951	2,205
Total stocks at historical cost	3,269	7,821	3,586	8,004
Current replacement cost exceeds the historical cost of stocks by	136	235	104	327

WHITE PLC
and its subsidiary companies
Notes to the Accounts — 31 March 1983 — continued

18   Debtors

	1983		1982	
	The company £'000	**The group** £'000	**The company** £'000	**The group** £'000
Amounts falling due within one year				
Trade debtors	2,370	6,774	2,655	6,416
Amounts owed by group companies:				
Subsidiaries	1,092	—	873	—
Other debtors — loan to a director (see (a) below)	6	6	6	6
Prepayments and accrued income	406	1,249	375	1,795
	3,874	8,029	3,909	8,217
Amounts falling due after one year				
Amounts owed by group companies:				
Fellow subsidiaries	500	—	500	—
Other debtors — loans to officers (see (b) below)	10	10	9	9
	510	10	509	9
	4,384	8,039	4,418	8,226

(a)   The loan to a director is a loan of £6,000 to Mr Walsh, the commercial director, necessary to enable him properly to perform his duties as an officer. The loan is unsecured, remained at £6,000 throughout the year, does not carry interest, and is repayable on demand.

(b)   Loans are outstanding in respect of three officers.

19   Other investments

Other investments relate to a holding of British government securities, with a market value of £183,000 (1982 — £270,000). These securities are listed on The Stock Exchange. Had the investments been realised at the year end at the above valuation, taxation of £5,000 (1982 — £7,000) would have become payable.

WHITE PLC
and its subsidiary companies
Notes to the Accounts — 31 March 1983 — continued

20   **Creditors — amounts falling due within one year**

	1983		1982	
	The company £'000	**The group** £'000	**The company** £'000	**The group** £'000
Debenture loans —$6\frac{1}{2}\%$ unsecured loan stock 1984 (see (a) below)	300	300	—	—
Bank loans and overdrafts (see (b) below)	95	336	42	420
Payments received on account	50	50	25	25
Trade creditors	1,424	3,657	2,652	5,381
Bills of exchange payable	125	198	232	296
Amounts owed to group companies:				
Subsidiaries	339	—	325	—
Holding company and fellow subsidiaries	297	—	186	—
Amounts owed to related companies	98	193	142	177
Other creditors including taxation and social security (see (c) below)	1,441	2,014	1,130	1,649
Accruals and deferred income	579	630	408	699
Dividends payable	678	678	678	678
	5,426	8,056	5,820	9,325

(a)   The $6\frac{1}{2}\%$ unsecured loan stock is redeemable at par on 1 January 1984.

(b)   The bank loans and overdrafts are secured by floating charges over the assets of the companies concerned.

(c)   'Other creditors including taxation and social security' is made up as follows:

	1983		1982	
	The company £'000	**The group** £'000	**The company** £'000	**The group** £'000
United Kingdom corporation tax:				
Payable 31 December	986	1,441	679	1,129
ACT on dividends	334	334	334	334
Overseas tax	4	30	18	12
	1,324	1,805	1,031	1,475
Social security	117	209	99	174
	1,441	2,014	1,130	1,649

WHITE PLC

and its subsidiary companies

Notes to the Accounts — 31 March 1983 — continued

21   **Creditors — amounts falling due after more than one year**

| | 1983 | | 1982 | |
	The company £'000	The group £'000	The company £'000	The group £'000
Debenture loans				
16% convertible unsecured loan stock 1991/96 (see (a) below)	200	200	200	200
$16\frac{1}{2}$% unsecured loan stock 1987 (see (b) below)	1,000	1,000	—	—
$14\frac{3}{4}$% unsecured loan stock 1988	—	700	—	700
$11\frac{1}{4}$% unsecured loan stock 1985	—	3,000	—	3,000
$6\frac{1}{2}$% unsecured loan stock 1984	—	—	—	300
	1,200	4,900	200	4,200
Bank loans and overdrafts				
7% unsecured loan repayable by annual instalments of £200,000 commencing in February 1990	800	800	800	800
Mortgages at $5\frac{3}{4}$% to 12% repayable by instalments falling due for payment between 1 January 1987 and 31 December 2001, and secured upon the freehold properties of the companies concerned	—	1,775	—	780
	800	2,575	800	1,580
Amounts owed to group companies — holding company and fellow subsidiaries				
4% unsecured loan 1988	600	—	600	—
6% unsecured loan 1985	400	—	400	—
	1,000	—	1,000	—
	3,000	7,475	2,000	5,780

WHITE PLC
and its subsidiary companies
Notes to the Accounts — 31 March 1983 — continued

(a) Each holder of the 16% convertible unsecured loan stock 1991/96 has the right, on the dates and at the rates set out below, on giving notice in writing during the month of February in each year, to convert his loan stock (being £1 stock or a multiple thereof) into ordinary shares of 25p each, fully paid, of White plc:

	Number of ordinary shares of 25p each receivable for every £100 loan stock
28 February 1987	200
28 February 1988	190
28 February 1989	180

(b) The $16\frac{1}{2}$% unsecured loan stock 1987 was issued at par during the year, and is redeemable for cash in 1987 at par. The issue was made so as to provide the company with working capital, at a time of heavy expenditure on new plant, and research and development, and also to help fund the purchase of Brown plc.

(c) All other debenture loans are redeemable for cash, at par, during the years indicated.

(d) An analysis of the loans by due date of repayment is set out below:

	1983		1982	
	The company £'000	The group £'000	The company £'000	The group £'000
Amounts payable more than five years hence, otherwise than by instalments:				
Debenture loans	200	900	200	900
Group companies	600	—	600	—
	800	900	800	900
Amounts payable by instalments, total instalments due more than five years hence:				
Bank loans	800	2,450	800	1,510
	800	2,450	800	1,510

WHITE PLC
and its subsidiary companies
Notes to the Accounts — 31 March 1983 — continued

	1983		1982	
	The company £'000	The group £'000	The company £'000	The group £'000
Loans due within five years:				
Between one and two years hence	400	—	—	300
Two and five years hence	1,000	4,125	400	3,070
	1,400	4,125	400	3,370
Total loans	3,000	7,475	2,000	5,780
The total value of loans repayable by instalments, any part of which falls due after more than five years, is	800	2,575	800	1,580

22   Pensions and similar obligations

The group schemes are non-contributory, and provide all employees with a pension on retirement. At the last actuarial valuation in 1981, one subsidiary's scheme was found to be underfunded. A provision of £151,000 (1982 — £103,000) has been established for the estimated amount of the deficiency. £48,000 was charged to profits and added to the provision during the year. A further valuation will be made next year, when a decision as to how the underfunding is to be made good will be taken.

23   Deferred taxation

Analysis of provision and potential liability:
The group

	1983		1982	
	Full potential liability £'000	Provision made £'000	Full potential liability £'000	Provision made £'000
Accelerated capital allowances	10,117	950	9,918	1,131
Capital gains rolled over	1,879	—	1,760	—
Other timing differences	(57)	(57)	(26)	(26)
	11,939	893	11,652	1,105
Less: ACT recoverable	(384)	(384)	(419)	(419)
	11,555	509	11,233	686

WHITE PLC
and its subsidiary companies
Notes to the Accounts — 31 March 1983 — continued

	1983		1982	
	Full potential liability £'000	Provision made £'000	Full potential liability £'000	Provision made £'000
The company				
Accelerated capital allowances	5,782	413	4,800	529
Other timing differences	(12)	(12)	6	6
	5,770	401	4,806	535
Less: ACT recoverable	(384)	(384)	(419)	(419)
	5,386	17	4,387	116

The major factors contributing to the restriction in the amounts provided are as follows:

(a) Accelerated tax allowance on plant and machinery. The group's medium term plans show that the amount of 100 per cent tax allowances in respect of eligible new plant to be acquired will fall short of the charge for depreciation on existing and new assets. Accordingly deferred tax is provided in respect of the estimated amount of this deficiency.

(b) The group has no intention of disposing of those properties against whose cost certain capital gains have been 'rolled over'. Were such a disposal to take place, it would in any case be necessary to repurchase a similar property, and accordingly further rollover relief would be available.

24 **Called up share capital**

	Ordinary shares of 25p each		5.6% redeemable cumulative preference shares of £1 each	
	1983 '000	1982 '000	1983 '000	1982 '000
Authorised:				
Value	£14,000	£14,000	£1,200	£1,200
Number	56,000	56,000	1,200	1,200
Issued, called up and fully paid:				
Value	£9,686	£9,686	£1,200	£1,200
Number	38,744	38,744	1,200	1,200

157

WHITE PLC
and its subsidiary companies
Notes to the Accounts — 31 March 1983 — continued

The preference shares may be redeemed, at the company's option, between 1 January 1990 and 31 December 1990 at a premium of 10p per share or, if still outstanding on 31 December 1990, must then be redeemed at par.

25 **Options on shares of White plc**

The following options have been granted and are still outstanding:

(a) To a director in respect of 10,000 ordinary shares of 25p each in White plc exercisable at any time before 1 December 1986, at a price of 55p per share.

(b) To the vendor of a business acquired by the group in respect of 45,000 ordinary shares in White plc exercisable at any time before 1 January 1985 at a price of 55p per share.

26 **Revaluation reserve**

The revaluation reserve arises as a consequence of carrying interests in land and buildings in the balance sheet at current replacement cost. The movement on the reserve is analysed below:

	£'000	£'000
At 1 April 1982		5,865
Exchange differences attributable to revaluation:		
On cost	198	
Depreciation	(175)	
		23
Revaluation in the year		636
		6,524
Revaluation surplus on properties disposed of, taken to the profit and loss account as realised extraordinary income		(261)
At 31 March 1983		6,263

No deferred tax has been provided in respect of this reserve because, in the opinion of the directors, sufficient rollover relief will be available to ensure that no liability to taxation will arise in the foreseeable future. The contingent liability is included in the potential liability to deferred tax set out in note 23.

WHITE PLC
and its subsidiary companies
Notes to the Accounts — 31 March 1983 — continued

27 **Profit and loss account**

The movement on consolidated retained profits is analysed below:

	White plc £'000	Subsidiary companies £'000	Related companies £'000	Total £'000
At 1 April 1982, as previously reported	5,415	5,187	49	10,651
Prior year adjustment (note 14(a))	(79)	(200)	—	(279)
As restated	5,336	4,987	49	10,372
Foreign currency translation gains	—	172	—	172
Retained profits for the year	130	262	50	442
At 31 March 1983	5,466	5,421	99	10,986
Retained for the year 1982	67	110	33	210

28 **Capital expenditure approved**

	1983		1982	
	The company £'000	The group £'000	The company £'000	The group £'000
Expenditure contracted for	250	600	1,530	2,280
Approved by the directors but not yet contracted for	170	290	2,090	2,580
Approved expenditure outstanding	420	890	3,620	4,860

Under present legislation, government grants estimated at £94,000 (1982 — £554,000) for the company and £168,000 (1982 — £642,000) for the group will be receivable in the future if all the above capital expenditure is incurred.

WHITE PLC
and its subsidiary companies
Notes to the Accounts — 31 March 1983 — continued

29   **Contingent liabilities and financial commitments**

	1983		1982	
	The company £'000	**The group** £'000	**The company** £'000	**The group** £'000
Amount of guarantees of bank overdrafts of related companies	200	400	350	550
Bills of exchange discounted	93	410	56	280
	293	810	406	830

(a)   There are no present indications that the group will be called on to honour its overdraft guarantees.

(b)   The discounted bills of exchange have all been drawn on major customers. Material loss is therefore considered unlikely. Should a loss arise corporation tax relief would be available.

(c)   The group has continuing financial commitments in respect of financing leases for plant and machinery. The total annual amount due under those leases extant at the balance sheet date was approximately £200,000, payable for the next seven years.

30   **Post balance sheet events**

Details of post balance sheet events are given in paragraph 2 of the directors' report.

WHITE PLC
and its subsidiary companies
Notes to the Accounts — 31 March 1983 — continued

31   **Group companies**

(a) The investment in subsidiaries is made up as follows:

	1983 £'000	1982 £'000
Investment at cost	8,119	7,460
Amortisation:		
At 1 April 1982	79	66
Charge for the year	14	13
At 31 March 1983	93	79
Net book value	8,026	7,381

The establishment of a provision against the cost of the company's investment in its subsidiaries is a consequence of the decision to amortise goodwill arising upon consolidation. The provision brought forward has been established by means of a prior year adjustment and restatement of the company's reserves.

(b) The directors consider that to give full particulars of all subsidiary companies would lead to a statement of excessive length. The following information relates to those subsidiaries which, in the opinion of the directors, principally affected the profits or assets of the group:

Name of company and country of incorporation and operation	Description of shares held	Proportion of nominal value of issued shares held	
		by White plc or its nominees %	by subsidiaries or their nominees %
Green plc (UK)*	Ordinary £1 shares	90	—
Blue plc (UK)	Ordinary 25p stock	100	—
Grey plc (UK)†	Ordinary £1 shares	10	60
Brown plc (UK)*	Ordinary £1 shares	100	—
Mauve Inc (USA)	Shares of no par value	70	—
Black GmbH (Germany)	Shares of DM 200	65	—

WHITE PLC
and its subsidiary companies
Notes to the Accounts — 31 March 1983 — continued

All the above companies operate principally in their country of incorporation.

†This company, which represents 13 per cent of the group's net assets, is not audited by Moorgate Place & Co.
*Registered in Scotland.

(c) The principal business activities of these subsidiaries are:
(i)   Green plc and Blue plc — manufacturers of precision electrical components.
(ii)   Grey plc — pressers of moulded plastics.
(iii) Brown plc and Mauve Inc — manufacturers of prefabricated building sections.
(iv) Black GmbH — manufacturers of domestic appliances.

32   **Ultimate holding company**

The directors regard Mega-White plc as the ultimate holding company. According to the register kept by the company, Mega-White plc had a 55 per cent interest in the equity capital of White plc.

Auditors' report page 127.

WHITE PLC
and its subsidiary companies

Consolidated Current Cost Accounts

1   Set out on pages 164 to 172 are supplementary accounts prepared by reference to current cost principles in conformity with Statement of Standard Accounting Practice No 16. Under this method of accounting, adjustments are made to the figures shown in the historical cost accounts to allow for the impact of price changes specific to the business when reporting assets employed and profits. Current cost accounts are not intended to demonstrate the effect of general inflation on the shareholders' interest in the business or to indicate the current value of the business.

2   In the balance sheet, stocks are stated at replacement cost and fixed assets are stated at depreciated replacement cost. Monetary items and deferred tax are as stated in the historical cost accounts. Investments in related companies and goodwill are restated on a current cost basis. The restatement of net assets in this way places a value in accounting terms on the operating capability of the business. Under current cost principles this operating capability has to be maintained before profit can be determined.

3   The current cost operating profit is the surplus on the ordinary activities of the business for the year, after making charges necessary to maintain the operating capability of that business. This involves four adjustments to the historical cost profit (see note B on page 168) as follows:

(a)   A cost of sales adjustment, to charge against profit the current cost of stocks as they are sold. This effectively provides the necessary funds to replace the stocks and so continue the business at a similar level.

(b)   A monetary working capital adjustment, to recognise the increase in funds required to finance debtors less creditors.

(c)   A depreciation adjustment, so that depreciation is computed on the current cost of fixed assets rather than historical cost.

(d)   A fixed asset disposal adjustment, to reflect the difference between the historical and current cost losses on the sale of fixed assets.

4   After determining the current cost operating profit, it is necessary to consider the impact of borrowings. Insofar as assets are partially financed and replaced by borrowed money, the full burden of price increases does not fall on the shareholders. To take account of this and so as to arrive at the current cost pre-tax profit, a further adjustment ('the gearing adjustment') is made whereby the net total of the four adjustments above is abated by the average proportion of the net operating assets that were financed by borrowings during the year.

5   The gearing and monetary working capital adjustments are taken to the current cost reserve. It is part of the concept of maintaining operating capability that this reserve should be treated as non-distributable. To use it to pay dividends would, in effect, mean returning to the shareholder the capital required for continuing operations at the present level.

WHITE PLC
and its subsidiary companies

Consolidated Current Cost Profit and Loss Account
for the year ended 31 March 1983

	Notes	1983 £'000	1982 £'000
Turnover		65,720	53,824
Historical cost of sales and operating expenses		62,526	50,830
Historical cost profit before interest, excluding attributable share of related companies' profits		3,194	2,994
Current cost operating adjustments	B	742	338
		2,452	2,656
Group's share of related companies' current cost profit before tax, but after interest and gearing	I	288	117
Current cost operating profit		2,740	2,773
Income from other fixed asset investments		274	94
Gearing adjustment	C	152	64
Interest on net borrowings		(734)	(639)
		(582)	(575)
Current cost profit before taxation		2,432	2,292
Taxation on profit on ordinary activities		1,449	1,298
Current cost profit on ordinary activities after taxation		983	994
Profit attributable to minority interests		170	143
Current cost profit after tax and before extraordinary item		813	851
Extraordinary item	D	284	
Current cost profit for the financial year attributable to the shareholders of White plc		1,097	851
Dividends paid or proposed		1,036	939
Retained current cost profit/deficit for the year		61	(88)
Current cost earnings per ordinary share	E	1.92p	2.02p

The notes on pages 168 to 172 form part of these accounts.
Auditors' report page 127.

WHITE PLC
and its subsidiary companies

Consolidated Current Cost Profit and Loss Account
for the year ended 31 March 1983 — continued

Statement of movements in reserves

	£'000	£'000
Reserves at 1 April 1982, as previously reported		16,472
Prior year adjustment (note 14(a) to the historical cost accounts)		(279)
Reserves at 1 April 1982, as restated		16,193
Exchange differences		227
		16,420
Retained current cost profit for the year	61	
Increase in current cost reserve for the year	971	
		1,032
Reserves at 31 March 1983		17,452

The notes on pages 168 to 172 form part of these accounts.
Auditors' report page 127.

WHITE PLC
and its subsidiary companies

Consolidated Current Cost Balance Sheet — 31 March 1983

	Notes	1983 £'000	1983 £'000	1982 £'000	1982 £'000
Fixed assets					
Intangible assets	H		1,597		1,408
Tangible assets	H		31,265		29,783
Investments:					
Shares in related companies	I	513		495	
Other investments other than loans		835		741	
			1,348		1,236
			34,210		32,427
Current assets					
Stocks		8,056		8,331	
Debtors		8,039		8,226	
Investments		183		270	
Cash at bank and in hand		561		336	
		16,839		17,163	
Creditors — amounts falling due after more than one year		8,056		9,325	
Net current assets			8,783		7,838
Total assets less current liabilities			42,993		40,265
Less: Non-current liabilities					
Creditors — amounts falling due after more than one year		7,475		5,780	
Provisions for liabilities and charges					
Deferred taxation		509		686	
Other provisions		151		103	
		660		789	
			8,135		6,569
			34,858		33,696

The notes on pages 168 to 172 form part of these accounts.
Auditors' report page 127.

WHITE PLC
and its subsidiary companies

Consolidated Current Cost Balance Sheet — 31 March 1983 — continued

	Notes	1983 £'000	1983 £'000	1982 £'000	1982 £'000
Capital and reserves					
Called up share capital		10,886		10,886	
Share premium account		1,512		1,512	
Current cost reserve	F	11,243		10,109	
Profit and loss account	G	6,209		6,084	
			29,850		28,591
Minority interests			5,008		5,105
			34,858		33,696

The notes on pages 168 to 172 form part of these accounts.
Auditors' report page 127.

WHITE PLC
and its subsidiary companies

Notes to the Current Cost Accounts — 31 March 1983

A   **Accounting policies**

(a)   The current cost accounts have been prepared in accordance with Statement of Standard Accounting Practice No 16 and, so far as practicable, the related guidance notes issued by the Accounting Standards Committee.

(b)   The accounting policies used in preparing the historical cost accounts have also been adopted in the current cost accounts. Foreign exchange differences arising on revalued assets are taken to the current cost reserve. All other foreign exchange differences are passed through the retained profit and loss account.

(c)   The current cost accounts are presented in summarised form. Further analyses of certain figures appearing in these accounts are contained in the historical cost accounts set out on pages 128 to 162. Where any figure appearing in the current cost accounts differs substantially from its equivalent in the historical cost accounts the nature of the difference is explained in the notes set out below. Brief explanations of the reasons for the salient adjustments made to the historical cost figures in order to arrive at their current cost equivalent are given on page 163.

B **Current cost operating adjustments**	1983 £'000	1982 £'000
Cost of sales adjustment (a)	100	83
Monetary working capital adjustment (b)	136	70
Total adjustment relating to working capital	236	153
Depreciation adjustment (c)	415	123
Fixed asset disposal adjustment (d)	91	62
Total adjustment relating to fixed assets	506	185
Total current cost operating adjustment	742	338

(a)   The cost of sales adjustment is the amount by which the current cost of goods sold differs from the historical cost. It is computed in accordance with the averaging method, using the mean price movements experienced by group companies during the year and taking account of the currencies in which particular stocks are purchased. Indices used are:

    (i)   in the United Kingdom, those published by the Central Statistical Office that most nearly correspond to the stocks held by the various group companies; and

    (ii)   overseas, the retail price index or nearest equivalent in each country concerned.

WHITE PLC
and its subsidiary companies

Notes to the Current Cost Accounts — 31 March 1983 — continued

(b) The adjustment in respect of monetary working capital has been calculated monthly by each group company, by reference to the same index as has been used in calculating the cost of sales adjustment. Monetary working capital for this purpose comprises trade debtors less trade creditors.

(c) The depreciation adjustment represents the difference between the depreciation charge in the historical cost accounts and the charge for the year calculated on the estimated current cost of the assets concerned. The restatement onto current cost of the accumulated depreciation arising in prior years ('backlog depreciation') has been charged to the current cost reserve.

(d) The adjustment on the disposal of fixed assets which are not treated as extraordinary items represents the difference between the historical and current cost net book values of the assets in question at the dates of disposal. The adjustment in respect of the extraordinary item is explained in note D.

C **Gearing adjustment**

The significance of the gearing adjustment and the method of calculation are described on page 163. For the purpose of calculating the gearing adjustment, the following figures have been used for borrowings and net operating assets:

	1983 £'000	1982 £'000
Borrowings comprise		
Long term loans:		
Non-current portion	7,475	5,780
Current portion	300	—
Deferred tax	509	686
Other provisions	151	103
Tax	1,805	1,475
Bank and cash balances and United Kingdom government securities, less overdrafts	(408)	(186)
	9,832	7,858
Net operating assets comprise		
Intangible fixed assets (see note H below)	1,597	1,408
Tangible fixed assets	31,265	29,783
Fixed asset investments	1,348	1,236
Stocks and work in progress	8,056	8,331
Monetary working capital (net)	2,424	796
	44,690	41,554

The average gearing proportion during the year applied to abate the current cost operating adjustment is 20.5 per cent (1982 — 18.9 per cent).

WHITE PLC
and its subsidiary companies

Notes to the Current Cost Accounts — 31 March 1983 — continued

D   Extraordinary item

The extraordinary profit (which is stated net of taxation and minority interests) arises from the disposal of freehold land and buildings and certain long leases.

E   Earnings per share

Current cost earnings per share are calculated by dividing the current cost profit attributable to shareholders before the extraordinary item [£813,000 (1982 — £851,000)], less preference dividends £67,200 (1982 — £67,200), by the 38,744,000 ordinary shares in issue throughout 1983 and 1982.

F   Current cost reserve

	£'000	£'000	£'000
Balance at 1 April 1982, as restated			10,109
Exchange differences on revalued assets			163
			10,272
Revaluation surpluses reflecting price changes:			
Intangible fixed assets	84		
Land and buildings	636		
Plant and machinery	56		
Fixed asset investments	82		
Stocks and work in progress	129		
		987	
Monetary working capital adjustment		136	
Gearing adjustment		(152)	
			971
Balance at 31 March 1983			11,243
Of which:			
Realised			2,951
Unrealised			8,292
			11,243

WHITE PLC
and its subsidiary companies

Notes to the Current Cost Accounts — 31 March 1983 — continued

(a) The realised element of this reserve represents the net cumulative difference between historical and current cost profits since current cost accounts were first prepared in 1980.

(b) No tax effect has been attributed to any of the transfers made to current cost reserve.

G   Retained profits

	£'000
Balance at 1 April 1982, as restated	6,084
Exchange differences other than on revalued assets	64
	6,148
Retained current cost profit	61
Balance at 31 March 1983	6,209

H   Fixed assets

		1983		1982
	Gross current cost £'000	Accumulated depreciation £'000	Net current cost £'000	Net current cost £'000
Intangible fixed assets	3,104	1,507	1,597	1,408
Tangible fixed assets:				
Land and buildings	14,838	3,229	11,609	10,780
Plant and machinery	37,968	18,312	19,656	19,003
	52,806	21,541	31,265	29,783
	55,910	23,048	32,862	31,191

(a) Intangible fixed assets, excluding goodwill, are stated at estimated current replacement cost. Goodwill is stated on the same basis as in the historical cost accounts.

WHITE PLC
and its subsidiary companies
Notes to the Current Cost Accounts — 31 March 1983 — continued

(b) Non-specialised land and buildings are stated at open market valuation at the balance sheet date, arrived at by the directors with, in some instances, the help of independent professional advice. The Derby factory was valued by George, Street & Co, a firm of independent chartered surveyors. The gross current cost of specialised buildings is computed in the same manner as for plant and equipment as described in (c) below.

(c) The gross current cost of plant and equipment is computed by applying indices to the historical cost. In the United Kingdom indices have been selected from those published by the Central Statistical Office; overseas, the retail price index or nearest equivalent in each country concerned has been used.

I **Related companies**

Current cost accounts have been prepared by the major related companies and the investment in related companies in the current cost accounts is included on this basis.

Auditors' report page 127.

WHITE PLC
and its subsidiary companies

Summary of the historical cost accounts for the five years ended 31 March 1983

	1979 £'000	1980 £'000	1981 £'000	1982 £'000	1983 £'000
Sales and results					
Turnover	41,772	45,312	50,629	53,824	65,720
Profit before taxation	1,879	2,013	2,514	2,609	3,054
Taxation	(1,031)	(1,020)	(1,492)	(1,298)	(1,449)
Profit after taxation	848	993	1,022	1,311	1,605
Minority interests	(87)	(98)	(151)	(162)	(411)
Profit after taxation, before extraordinary items	761	895	871	1,149	1,194
Extraordinary items	—	(136)	—	—	284
Attributable profit	761	759	871	1,149	1,478
Dividends	(483)	(466)	(722)	(939)	(1,036)
Retained profit	278	293	149	210	442
Net assets employed					
Fixed assets	23,889	25,164	28,970	30,330	32,030
Net current assets	5,436	7,803	6,959	7,488	8,531
	29,325	32,967	35,929	37,818	40,561
Non-current liabilities	(1,986)	(6,358)	(5,235)	(5,780)	(7,475)
Provisions for liabilities and charges, including deferred tax	(655)	(747)	(612)	(789)	(660)
	26,684	25,862	30,082	31,249	32,426
Ratios					
Profit before taxation as a percentage of sales	4.5%	4.4%	5.0%	4.8%	4.6%
Profit before taxation as a percentage of net assets employed	7.0%	7.8%	8.4%	8.3%	9.4%
Earnings per ordinary share	1.79p	2.14p	2.07p	2.79p	2.91p
Dividends per ordinary share	1.07p	1.03p	1.69p	2.25p	2.50p

Note
The figures for 1979 to 1982 have been adjusted to reflect the accounting policy now adopted in respect of goodwill.

WHITE PLC
and its subsidiary companies

Summary of the current cost accounts for the five years ended 31 March 1983

	1979 £'000	1980 £'000	1981 £'000	1982 £'000	1983 £'000
Sales and results					
Turnover	41,772	45,312	50,629	53,824	65,720
Current cost profit before taxation	1,566	1,873	2,195	2,292	2,432
Taxation	(1,031)	(1,020)	(1,492)	(1,298)	(1,449)
Profit after taxation	535	853	703	994	983
Minority interests	(125)	(136)	(139)	(143)	(170)
Profit after taxation, before extraordinary items	410	717	564	851	813
Extraordinary items	—	(136)	—	—	284
Attributable profit	410	581	564	851	1,097
Dividends	(483)	(466)	(722)	(939)	(1,036)
Retained profit/loss	(73)	115	(158)	(88)	61
Net assets employed					
Fixed assets	28,412	31,949	31,638	32,427	34,210
Net current assets	5,690	8,168	7,284	7,838	8,783
	34,102	40,117	38,922	40,265	42,993
Non-current liabilities	(1,986)	(6,358)	(5,235)	(5,780)	(7,475)
Provisions for liabilities and charges, including deferred tax	(655)	(747)	(612)	(789)	(660)
	31,461	33,012	33,075	33,696	34,858
Ratios					
Profit before taxation as a percentage of sales	3.7%	4.1%	4.3%	4.3%	3.7%
Profit before taxation as a percentage of net assets employed	5.0%	5.7%	6.6%	6.8%	7.0%
Earnings per ordinary share	0.88p	1.68p	1.28p	2.02p	1.92p
Dividends per ordinary share	1.07p	1.03p	1.69p	2.25p	2.50p

Note

The figures for 1979 to 1982 have been adjusted to reflect the accounting policy now adopted in respect of goodwill.

WHITE PLC
and its subsidiary companies

Summary of key ratios for the five years ended 31 March 1983

Current cost accounts are concerned with the effect on the group of price changes specific to the group. As such they are not intended to demonstrate the effect of general inflation on the shareholders' interest in the business.

Some indication of this later aspect can be derived by indexing amounts by reference to the retail price index. The following table illustrates this in respect of shareholders' interests in assets, profits and dividends:

	1979 p	1980 p	1981 p	1982 p	1983 p
Net assets per share					
On historical cost basis:					
As shown in accounts adjusted to 1983 price levels	68.9	66.8	77.6	80.7	83.7
On current cost basis:					
As shown in accounts adjusted to 1983 price levels	81.2	85.2	85.4	87.0	90.0
Earnings per share					
On historical cost basis:					
As shown in accounts adjusted to 1983 price levels	1.79	2.14	2.07	2.79	2.91
On current cost basis:					
As shown in accounts adjusted to 1983 price levels	0.88	1.68	1.28	2.02	1.92
Dividends per share					
As shown in accounts adjusted to 1983 price levels	1.07	1.03	1.69	2.25	2.50

Note
The figures for 1979 to 1982 have been adjusted to reflect the accounting policy now adopted in respect of goodwill.

Appendix 3 — Mini-White Limited

Mini-White Limited is designed to provide an example of the accounts of a simple group, modified for filing with the registrar of companies under the 'small company' provisions.

The Mini-White Limited accounts are drawn up for the year to 31 March 1983 because it is unlikely that the requirements of the Companies Act 1981 will become applicable before 1982/83.

Report of the auditors to the directors of Mini-White Limited

1 In our opinion the requirements for exemption as a small company, as defined by section 7(8) of the Companies Act 1981, are satisfied in relation to the attached modified accounts. We are not required to express an audit opinion on these modified accounts.

2 We reported, as auditors of Mini-White Limited, to the members on 19 June 1983 on the company's financial statements prepared under section 1 of the Companies Act 1976 for the year ended 31 March 1983 as follows:

We have audited the accounts set out on pages 3 to 20 in accordance with approved Auditing Standards. These accounts have been prepared under the historical cost convention modified by the revaluation of certain fixed assets.

In our opinion these accounts give a true and fair view of the state of affairs of the company and of the group at 31 March 1983 and of the profit and source and application of funds of the group for the year then ended and comply with the Companies Acts 1948 to 1981.

Moorgate Place & Co
Chartered Accountants

London, 25 June 1983

MINI-WHITE LIMITED
and its subsidiary company

Consolidated Balance Sheet — 31 March 1983
(Modified in accordance with the provisions of the Companies Act 1981)

	Notes	1983 £'000	1983 £'000	1982 £'000	1982 £'000
Fixed assets					
Intangible assets		23		23	
Tangible assets		547		528	
			570		551
Current assets					
Stocks		251		173	
Debtors (all due within one year)	2	153		168	
Cash at bank and in hand		15		7	
		419		348	
Creditors — amounts falling due within one year		(317)		(256)	
Net current assets			102		92
Total assets less current liabilities			672		643
Less: Non-current liabilities					
Creditors — amounts falling due after more than one year	3	200		200	
Provision for liabilities and charges		79		68	
			279		268
			393		375
Capital and reserves					
Called up share capital	4		50		50
Share premium account			25		25
Revaluation reserve			71		71
Profit and loss account			247		229
			393		375

S WHITE
S DWARFS } Directors

The notes on pages 179 and 180 form part of these accounts.
Auditors' report page 176

MINI-WHITE LIMITED
Balance Sheet — 31 March 1983
(Modified in accordance with the provisions of the Companies Act 1981)

	Notes	1983 £'000	1983 £'000	1982 £'000	1982 £'000
Fixed assets					
Tangible assets		490		483	
Investment (note 5)	5	50		50	
			540		533
Current assets					
Stocks		251		173	
Debtors (all due within one year)	2	95		111	
Cash at bank and in hand		10		4	
		356		288	
Creditors — amounts falling due within one year		(318)		(270)	
Net current assets			38		18
Total assets less current liabilities			578		551
Less: Non-current liabilities					
Creditors — amounts falling due after more than one year	3	200		200	
Provision for liabilities and charges		75		67	
			275		267
			303		284
Capital and reserves					
Called up share capital	4		50		50
Share premium account			25		25
Revaluation revenue			71		71
Profit and loss account			157		138
			303		284

In preparing these modified accounts we have relied upon the exemptions for individual accounts, contained in the Companies Act 1981. We have done so on the grounds that the company is entitled to the benefit of those exemptions, as a small company. By virtue of section 10 of the same Act, the documents delivered to the registrar will include copies of modified group accounts.

S WHITE ⎫
S DWARFS ⎬ Directors

The notes on pages 179 and 180 form of part of these accounts.
Auditors' report page 176.

MINI-WHITE LIMITED
and its subsidiary company

Notes to the Modified Accounts — 31 March 1983

1   **Principal accounting policies**

(a) **Basis of consolidation**

The consolidated accounts include the company and its subsidiary. Intra group sales and profits are eliminated on consolidation, and all sales and profit figures relate to external transactions only.

The excess of the purchase price over the value of the net assets of the subsidiary company is included in the consolidated balance sheet under intangible assets.

(b) **Depreciation**

Depreciation is calculated so as to write off the cost of fixed assets on a straight line basis over the expected useful lives of the assets concerned. The principal annual rates used for this purpose, which are consistent with those of last year, are:

	%
Freehold buildings	2
Precision plant	25
Other plant	10
Motor vehicles	25
Furniture, fixtures and fittings	15

No provision for depreciation is made against goodwill arising on consolidation.

(c) **Foreign currencies**

Assets and liabilities expressed in foreign currencies are translated to sterling at the rates of exchange ruling at the end of the financial year.

(d) **Stocks and work in progress**

Stocks and work in progress are stated at the lower of cost and net realisable value. In general, cost is determined on a first in first out basis and includes transport and handling costs; in the case of manufactured products cost includes all direct expenditure and production overheads based on the normal level of activity. Net realisable value is the price at which the stocks can be sold in the normal course of business after allowing for the costs of realisation and, where appropriate, the cost of conversion from their existing state to a finished condition. Provision is made where necessary for obsolescent, slow moving and defective stocks.

(e) **Deferred taxation**

Provision is made for deferred tax at the rate of corporation tax ruling at the year end (the 'liability method'), except in respect of any tax reduction which can reasonably be expected to continue for the foreseeable future.

MINI-WHITE LIMITED
and its subsidiary company

Notes to the Modified Accounts — 31 March 1983 — continued

(f) **Warranties for products**

Provision is made for the estimated liability on all products still under warranty, including claims already received.

2 **Loan to a director**

Included in debtors is an amount of £6,000, which is a loan to the managing director, Mr White. The loan, which was made to enable him to meet expenditure incurred on the company's business, remained at £6,000 for the whole of the year, and is unsecured. It does not bear interest, and is repayable on demand.

3 **Creditors — amounts falling due after more than one year**

This liability comprises £200,000 of 10% loan stock, repayable on 31 March 1990. The loan is secured by a floating charge over the assets of the company.

4 **Called up share capital**

	1983	1982
Authorised, issued, called up and fully paid ordinary shares of £1 each: Number	50,000	50,000
Value	£50,000	£50,000

5 **Investment**

The investment represents the cost of the company's 100 per cent interest in its subsidiary, Mini-White (Marketing) Limited.

	1983	1982
50,000 ordinary shares of £1 each, at cost	£50,000	£50,000

6 **Profit of Mini-White Limited**

The profit for the year retained by Mini-White Limited was £16,000 (1982 — £14,000).

Auditors' report page 176.

Appendix 4   Disclosure Requirements Checklist

The purpose of this checklist is to provide a convenient means of determining whether or not a set of accounts complies with the disclosure provisions of the Companies Acts, SSAPs and the Listing Agreement. Although the checklist is a complete tabulation of the legal and other requirements it is of necessity a summarisation. In cases of doubt as to the meaning of any requirement, reference should be made to the appropriate place in the text, indicated by the chapter and paragraph references in the middle column below.

It should be noted that this checklist is not applicable to companies preparing accounts that follow schedule 8A to the Companies Act 1981, and that it does not contain the special provisions relating to investment companies.

When used in practice, this checklist should have one or two columns (one for the company and one for the group) included on the right hand side, so that ticks can be inserted in the appropriate column(s) as items are checked.

DIRECTORS' REPORT

General

1948 s 157(1)	2.1	Directors' report to be attached to balance sheet.
1967 s 23A (per 1981 s 15)	2.32	Auditors to report if directors' report inconsistent with accounts.

Disclosure

1967 s 16(1)	2.3	Principal activities and significant changes during the year.
1948 s 157(1) (per 1981 s 13(1))	2.4–5	Fair review of the development of business in the year and year end position.
LA para 10(b)	2.6	Explanation of material differences from published forecasts.
1967 s 16(1)(f)(ii) (per 1981 s 13(3))	2.7	Likely future developments in business.
1948 s 157(1)	2.9	Proposed dividend and transfers to reserves.
1967 s 16(1)(a)	2.10	Significant changes in fixed assets.
1967 s 16(1)(a)	2.11	Estimate of market value of land and buildings if substantially different from book value.

1967 s 16(1)(f)(i) (per 1981 s 13(3)) SSAP 17:23–25 Author	2.13–17	Details of material post balance sheet events as follows: (a) full details of material adjusting and non-adjusting events; and (b) details of reversal or maturity of transactions entered into to alter the appearance of the balance sheet. State nature of event, estimate of effect and tax implications.
1967 s 16(1)(f)(iii) (per 1981 s 13(3))	2.18	Indication of group research and development activities, if any.
SI 1980 No 1160	2.20	If on average more than 250 employees working wholly or mainly in UK during year, state policy on employment, training and advancement of disabled persons, and policy on continuing the employment of persons becoming disabled during their employment.
1967 s 16(1)(g)	2.21	Group health, safety and welfare at work arrangements (not as yet required but Secretary of State can make orders).
1967 s 16(1)	2.22	Names of directors serving at any time in the year.
LA para 11(d)	2.22	Unexpired period of service agreements of directors standing for re-election (not applicable to USM companies).
1967 s 16(1)(e), 27, 31 1967 s 16(4) 1967 s 16(4A) (per 1981 s 13(4)) SI 1967 No 1594 SI 1968 No 865, 1533 LA para 10(h)	2.23–25	State each director's interests in shares or debentures of every group company (specifying the company) and number and amount of each. Show nil holdings and comparatives at start of year, or date of appointment if later. See 2.24 for exemptions. If listed, show split between beneficial and other holdings, and changes in holdings after year end in period up to one month before notice of general meeting is given. If no such changes, state that fact. Information may alternatively be given in notes to the accounts.
LA para 10(n)	2.26	Waivers of dividends by shareholders.
LA para 10(i)	2.27–28	Holdings of the company's share capital in excess of 5 per cent. If none, state none.
1967 S19 SI 1980 No 1055	2.19	If total of political and charitable contributions (excepting those made to persons or parties outside the UK) exceeds £200, show separate totals. Name recipients of individual

political donations in excess of £200 and state amount. However:

(a) above disclosures do not apply to wholly owned subsidiary of company incorporated in Great Britain; and

(b) if a company has subsidiaries, and is not exempted by (a) above, disclose details for group as a whole instead.

1967 s 16A   2.29   Where a company's shares:
(per 1981 s 14)

(a) are acquired by that company by purchase, forfeiture or surrender; or

(b) are acquired through a nominee, or through a person who has obtained financial assistance from the company in circumstances in which the company has a beneficial interest in the shares; or

(c) are made subject to a lien or other charge taken by that company;

show the number, nominal value and percentage of called up capital that each of the following represents:

(i)   Shares purchased (and state consideration and reasons for purchase).
(ii)   Shares acquired by a nominee or by the company, or subject to a lien or charge.
(iii)   The maximum holding acquired by the company or its nominee, or charged, at any time during the year.
(iv)   Shares so acquired or charged and disposed of or cancelled in the year.

Where shares are charged, state the amount of the charge. Where shares are disposed of, state consideration.

LA para 10(j)   2.30   State whether or not close company provisions of ICTA 1970
Author   (as amended) apply, and whether there has been any change in this respect since previous year.

Author   2.31   Reference to resolution to reappoint auditors.

FORMAT RULES

1981 1 sch 1, 3(3)	3.1–7	Balance sheet and profit and loss account to follow standard format, subject to options available. Items to be shown in order, and under headings, specified.
Author	3.8	Headings in the standard formats may not be abbreviated.
1981 1 sch 2(1)–(2)	3.9	Standard format to be consistently adopted. Particulars and reasons for any changes to be disclosed.
1981 1 sch 3(1)	3.10	Items may be shown in greater detail if required.
1981 1 sch 3(2)	3.11 5.92	Additional items may be included if required, except that the following may never be treated as assets:

(a) Preliminary expenses.
(b) Expenses or commission on issue of shares or debentures.
(c) Research costs.

1981 1 sch 3(4)	3.12, 18	Items indicated in standard formats by Arabic numerals may be combined if immaterial or where their combination facilitates assessment of accounts. In latter case, show detail in notes.
1981 1 sch 4(1)–(2) 1981 1 sch 58(2)	3.13–14	Comparatives to be shown throughout the accounts and notes unless contrary indicated. If not comparable, adjust corresponding amount and explain and state effect in notes.
1981 1 sch 5	3.15	Assets and liabilities, income and expenditure, are not to be netted off.
1981 1 sch 3(3)	3.6	Subheadings with Arabic numerals may be rearranged if nature of business requires it.
1981 1 sch 3(5), 4(3)	3.17	Headings for which there are nil balances in both current and prior year to be omitted.
1981 1 sch 85	3.19	Disclosure requirements of 1981 1 sch may be disregarded for immaterial amounts.

True and Fair View

1948 s 149(2)–(4) (per 1981 s 1(1)) 1948 s 152(2)–(3) (per 1981 s 2)	3.16 8.2	Overriding requirement for accounts to show true and fair view. Directors must therefore, if necessary: (a) include additional information; (b) depart from standard formats and disclosure rules and state reasons and effects.

ACCOUNTING PRINCIPLES AND POLICIES

1981 1 sch 15 SSAP 2:17	4.4	If accounts do not comply with any of the four fundamental accounting concepts (i.e. going concern, consistency, matching and accruals) state by note: (a) particulars of departure; (b) reasons for it; and (c) effect.
1981 1 sch 36 SSAP 2:18	4.6, 19	State accounting policies in respect of material items, and in particular explain policies for:
1981 1 sch 58(1) SSAP 6:6		(a) foreign currency translation;
1981 1 sch 36 SSAP 12:22		(b) depreciation and diminution of assets; and
Author		(c) goodwill.
SSAP — Explanatory Foreword LA para 10(a)	4.7	Give explanations for significant departures from SSAPs.
1981 1 sch 28, 51(1)	4.12	If no record of purchase price or production cost of asset exists, use the earliest available information and state facts when this provision is first applied.
1981 1 sch 24	4.13	If amount repayable on a debt exceeds consideration received, and excess is treated as an asset, show by note unamortised amount of asset if not shown on face of balance sheet.

185

BALANCE SHEET

General

See format section 1981 sch 1 format notes	5.1	Balance sheet to follow one of the specified formats. If headings are combined on the face of the balance sheet, they are to be set out in full in the notes. Certain alternative positions are permitted for captions. These are referred to under the relevant headings.
1981 1 sch 59	5.2	If company is holding company or subsidiary, for each item in either balance sheet format requiring disclosure of balances related to group companies, give separate totals (either by note, or on face of balance sheet) for amounts attributable to dealings with:

(a)   holding company and fellow subsidiaries; and
(b)   subsidiaries.

1981 1 sch 67

Equivalent disclosure in consolidated accounts required for balances attributable to unconsolidated subsidiaries.

Fixed Assets

General

1981 1 sch 42(1)–(2)	5.6	For each item shown as a fixed asset (whether tangible, intangible or investment) disclose:

(a)   cost, revaluation, or current cost at beginning of year and balance sheet date;
(b)   revaluations in year;
(c)   acquisitions in year;
(d)   disposals in year;
(e)   transfers to or from that item;

1981 1 sch 42(3)   5.7   and in respect of depreciation:

(f)   accumulated depreciation at beginning of year and balance sheet date;
(g)   charge for the year and provisions for diminutions;
(h)   adjustments for disposals;
(i)   other adjustments.

1981 1 sch 58(3)	5.8	Comparatives are not required, for the statements at 5.6 and 5.7 above, except by way of the opening figures for costs and depreciation.

SSAP 12:19–22	5.9	For each major class of depreciated asset, show:

(a) depreciation method used;
(b) useful lives or depreciation rates used;
(c) effect on depreciation, in year of change of:

    (i) change in method of depreciation; or
    (ii) revaluation of fixed assets.

1981 1 sch 29–34	5.10	Where any fixed assets are included at a revalued amount, give the further information required by the alternative accounting rules.
1981 1 sch 26(3)(b) LA para 10(g)	5.11–12	If interest on funds borrowed to finance the production of an asset has been included in that asset's production cost, disclose the amount of interest by note to the accounts. Listed companies to state amount and treatment of any related tax relief.

Fixed Assets — Intangibles

Development costs

1981 1 sch 20(1)–(2) SSAP 13:21	5.13	These may only be included in the balance sheet in special circumstances. In which case state:

(a) period over which they are to be written off; and
(b) reason for capitalisation.

SSAP 13:29	5.14	The accounting policy followed is to be clearly explained.
1980 s 42A (per 1981 s 84)	5.15	If development expenses not treated as realised loss in computing distributable profits, state reason by note.

Concessions, patents, licences, trade marks etc

1981 1 sch format note 2	5.16	Such assets may only be included in the balance sheet if either:

(a) not 'goodwill' and acquired for valuable consideration; or
(b) created by company itself.

Goodwill (other than that arising on consolidation)

1981 1 sch format note 3	5.18	Goodwill only to be included if acquired for valuable consideration.
1981 1 sch 21(2)–(4)	5.19–20	Goodwill is to be systematically written off over a period chosen by directors, not longer than its useful economic life. Period, and reason for choosing it, to be disclosed by note.

Fixed Assets — Tangibles

General

1981 1 sch 25(1)–(2)	5.28	Tangibles of a kind which are constantly being replaced may be included in balance sheet at a fixed quantity and value, provided not material.

Land and buildings

1981 1 sch 44, 82	5.23–24	Show separately:

(a) freehold land and buildings;
(b) long leases, with 50 or more years to run;
(c) short leases, with less than 50 years to run.

Investment properties

SSAP 19:15	5.26	Carrying value of investment properties to be prominently displayed.
1981 1 sch 43 SSAP 19:12	5.27	Names or qualifications of valuers to be disclosed, together with bases of valuation. If valuer is officer or employee of group, state that fact.

Investments

General

Author	5.29	Investments may be included as either fixed or current assets.
1981 1 sch 45(1)	5.31	Wherever shown, investments are to be split between listed and other investments. Listed investments are to be distinguished between those listed on a recognised stock exchange and others.
1981 1 sch 45(2)	5.33	For listed investments, state aggregate market value if different from accounts value. If, for purpose of accounts, market value is taken to be higher than stock exchange value, also state latter.
Author	5.32	Consider analysing securities listed overseas according to location of principal market in their shares.
1981 1 sch 27(3)–(5)	5.37	For fungible investments state any material difference between value in accounts and replacement cost or most recent purchase price.

Own shares

1981 1 sch format note 4	5.38	Show separately nominal value of own shares held, as either item **BIII** 7 or **CIII** 2.

Tax certificates of deposit

Author	5.62	Show separately tax certificates of deposit, normally as current assets at item CIII 3.

Other matters in respect of investments
Investments in companies that are not subsidiaries

1967 s 4(1)–(2)   5.57–58   If the investment exceeds:
1967 s 4(1A)   Category A
(per 1981 s 3(1))

(a)   one-tenth of any class of the investee's equity share capital; or
(b)   one-tenth of investee's allotted share capital; or
(c)   one-tenth of investor's assets; then

state in notes, in respect of investee:

(d)   name;
(e)   country of incorporation, but if Great Britain state country of registration if different from investor company;

1981 1 sch 58(3)   (f)   description and proportion of nominal value of issued share capital of each class held. Comparative figures are not required.

1967 s 4(3)   5.60   Disclosure above is not required for investments in companies incorporated or carrying on business outside the UK, if disclosure would be harmful and provided Department of Trade approval is given.

1967 s 4(4)   5.60   If this information would be of excessive length, give details only of those investments directors consider most material and state only limited disclosure made. No information need be given in respect of investments included in consolidated accounts, although the holding company must give details of its own investments in the notes to its own balance sheet.

1981 s 4(2)–(3)   5.57–58   If the investment exceeds one-fifth of the allotted share capital
                    Category B   of the investee company show, in addition to the disclosures above:

(a)   the aggregate capital and reserves of the investee company at its most recent year end; and

189

		(b) its profit or loss for the most recent financial year.
1981 s 4(5)–(7)	5.59	However, this additional information is not required if:

(a) the investment is less than 50 per cent of the nominal value of the allotted share capital of the investee, and that investee is not required to file its balance sheet with the registrar, and does not publish its balance sheet anywhere in the world; or

(b) it is not material; or

(c) the investment is included in the accounts by way of the equity method of valuation.

1981 1 sch 63(b), (d), 68	5.58	The above disclosures in respect of companies that are not subsidiaries need be made only in the accounts of the investor company, and not in any group accounts.
SSAP 1:6, 21	5.58 Category C	In the case of investor companies where the group interest exceeds 20 per cent of the equity capital state the name of the investee, and the description and proportion of the nominal value of issued shares held. Comparatives are not required.

If the investor is listed state in addition in respect of the investee:

LA para 10(e)	5.58	(a) principal country of operation;

(b) details of issued share and loan capital, and total reserves, unless dealt with as a related company;

(c) investing group's interest in each class of loan capital (direct and indirect).

Associated (or related) companies

The disclosure requirements above must be followed. In addition, the following provisions are relevant:

SSAP 1:19	5.52–53	(a) Unless shown at a valuation, in group balance sheet show related companies at cost, less amounts written off, plus group share of post acquisition retained reserves.
SSAP 1:19	5.53	(b) If no subsidiaries, or no consolidated accounts, share of post acquisition reserves to be shown by note.

SSAP 1:19	5.58	(c) Information about related company assets and liabilities to be given if materially relevant to assessment of nature of investment.
SSAP 1:20	5.55	(d) Consolidated retained reserves to show separately share of related companies' post acquisition retained profits and movement on other reserves. Specify effect of any further tax on distribution of retained reserves from overseas associates.
SSAP 1:21	5.50	(e) Names and details of interest in related companies, and those in which more than 20 per cent held, but not treated as related companies.
SSAP 1:12	5.54	(f) The reasons for omitting any related company's results from the group accounts to be stated.
SSAP 1:11	5.54	(g) If the accounts of a related company are unaudited, or not coterminous, the facts and accounting dates are to be shown.
SSAP 1:19	5.58	(h) Give summary of tangible and intangible assets of related company if necessary for a fair understanding of nature of investment.

Investments in subsidiary companies

1967 s 3(1)	5.42	Show by note in respect of each subsidiary:
		(a) name;
		(b) country of incorporation if not Great Britain. If Great Britain, state country of registration if different from that of holding company;
1967 s 3(1)–(2) SSAP 14:33 1981 1 sch 58(3)		(c) description and proportion of nominal value of issued shares of each class held, distinguishing between direct and indirect holdings. Corresponding figures for previous year not required;
1981 s 4(3)(a)		(d) aggregate capital and reserves at most recent year end (holding company accounts only);
1981 s 4(3)(b)		(e) profit or loss for most recent year (holding company accounts only);

SSAP 14:33

(f) indication of nature of business (principal subsidiaries only);

LA para 10(d)

(g) if holding company listed, state principal country of operations of material, active subsidiaries.

1981 s 4(4)   5.43

Information in (d) and (e) above is not required if:

(a) the holding company is exempt from preparing group accounts; or

(b) the holding company prepares group accounts and either:

    (i) the subsidiary is included therein; or
    (ii) the investment in the subsidiary is included in the holding company's accounts under the equity method of accounting; or

1981 s 4(5)

(c) the investment is included in, or in a note to, the company's accounts by way of the equity method of valuation; or

1981 s 4(6)

(d) the holding company has less than 50 per cent of the subsidiary (i.e. investee is subsidiary by virtue of 1948 s 154(1)(a)(i), control of board) and:

    (i) the subsidiary is not required to publish its balance sheet anywhere in the world; and
    (ii) it is not required to file its balance sheet with the registrar; or

1981 s 4(7)

(e) it is immaterial.

1967 s 3(4)–(5)   5.44

If, in the opinion of the directors, the above requirements would result in particulars of excessive length, they may restrict information to those subsidiaries principally affecting the group's accounts, provided that existence of such omissions is disclosed.

1967 s 3(3)   5.45

In certain circumstances the Department of Trade may sanction the omission of certain subsidiaries from all the above requirements.

SSAP 14:18   5.46

If length of a principal subsidiary's accounting period is different from that of holding company, state length of period.

1981 1 sch 70 SSAP 14:18	5.46	If subsidiary companies have year ends which are not coterminous with holding company, state:

(a) reason for different accounting dates;
(b) the accounting dates, or earliest and latest accounting dates, used;
(c) names of subsidiaries involved.

1981 1 sch 60	5.48	If a subsidiary holds beneficially shares or debentures in its holding company, the holding company is to state by note the number, description and amount of such shares or debentures.

Debentures of the company

1981 1 sch 41(3)	5.61	Nominal amount and book value of debentures of the company held by a nominee or trustee for the company.

Current Assets

Stocks

1981 1 sch 23(1) SSAP 9:26–27	5.63, 69	Stocks and work in progress (excluding long term contracts) to be stated at lower of cost and net realisable value. Long term contracts to be stated at cost plus attributable profits, less foreseeable losses, less progress payments received and receivable.

SSAP 9:27, 30	5.69	Disclose separately in respect of long term contracts:

(a) cost plus attributable profits, less foreseeable losses; and
(b) progress payments received and receivable.

Excess losses should be shown separately as provisions at item E9.

SSAP 9:11, 28	5.65	State accounting policy followed in respect of stocks in general, and particularly in respect of 'cost', 'net realisable value' and 'attributable profits'.
SSAP 9:29	5.63	Stocks and work in progress should be classified in the balance sheet under headings appropriate to the business.
SSAP 9:12	5.64	If different types of stocks have been valued on different bases, state amounts included in accounts for each type.
1981 1 sch 25	5.70	'Raw materials and consumables' may be included in the accounts at a fixed quantity and value provided that:

(a) the amounts are immaterial; and
(b) the amounts are not subject to material variation.

| 1981 1 sch 27(1)–(2) | 5.66 | Cost to be determined on the basis considered appropriate by directors, to be one of: |

(a) LIFO;
(b) FIFO;
(c) weighted average; or
(d) similar method.

| 1981 1 sch 27(3)–(5) | 5.71 | If stocks are stated at an amount materially different from current replacement cost or most recent purchase or production cost, state amount of difference by note. |

| Author | 5.68 | If material amount of stocks held subject to suppliers' reservation of title claims state facts and amounts involved. |

Debtors

| 1981 1 sch format note 5 | 5.72 | Amounts falling due after more than one year to be shown separately for each item included under debtors. |

| 1981 1 sch format note 6 | 5.73 | Prepayments and accrued income may be shown in either of the positions shown in the formats. |

Financial assistance for acquisition of own shares

| 1981 1 sch 51(2) | 5.90 | If company has given financial assistance for purchase of its own or holding company's shares: |

(a) under an employee share scheme;
1981 s 42(6)(b)   (b) to employees, other than directors; or
1981 s 42(6)(c)   (c) (by private companies) under 1981 s 43;
1981 s 43

state separately aggregate amount of such loans included in any balance sheet item.

Loans to, and other transactions with, directors

5.74–5.89   Companies (other than recognised banks or their holding companies) to show particulars of transactions or arrangements falling within section 49, Companies Act 1980 (principally loans, guarantees, the provision of security, quasi-loans and credit transactions) between the company (or its subsidiary) and a director (or connected person) of the company or of its holding company, or of any agreements to make such transactions or arrangements, and of any other transactions or arrangements in which a director (or connected person) had (at any time in the year) a material interest. Comparative figures are not required.

1981 1 sch 58(3)

1980 s 54(5), 55(1)	5.83	Companies (other than recognised banks or their holding companies) to give the following particulars of a transaction, arrangement or agreement to be disclosed in respect of items referred to above:

1980 s 55(1)(a)

(a) A statement that it was made or subsisted (whichever applies) during the year.

1980 s 55(1)(b)–(c)

(b) Names of directors (and, where relevant, connected persons) concerned and, for transactions to which section 54(1)(c) or section 54(2)(c) of the Companies Act 1980 applies, the nature of the directors' interests.

1980 s 55(1)
Author

(c) Principal terms (including those relating to repayment, interest and security).

1980 s 55(1)(d)

(d) For loans, or agreements for or arrangements relating to loans:

　　(i)　the amount of the liability (principal and interest) at the beginning and end of the year;
　　(ii)　the maximum amount of that liability during the year;
　　(iii)　the amounts of any arrears of interest;
　　(iv)　any provision against non-repayment of the whole or any part of the principal or interest.

1980 s 55(1)(e)

(e) For guarantees or the provision of security, or agreements or arrangements relating thereto:

　　(i)　the amount for which the company (or its subsidiary) was liable at the beginning and end of the year;
　　(ii)　the maximum amount in which the company (or its subsidiary) may become so liable;
　　(iii)　any amount paid or liability incurred in fulfilling the guarantee or discharging the security.

1980 s 55(1)(f)

(f) For any other transaction, arrangement or agreement, the value of the transaction or arrangement.

Notes:

5.85　　1. The following are exempted from the disclosure requirements set out above:

1980 s 54(6)(b)		(a) Service contracts between a company and a director or a director of its holding company.

1980 s 54(6)(a)

(b) Transactions, arrangements or agreements between two companies where a director is only interested by virtue of being a director of both companies.

1980 s 58(1)–(2)

(c) Transactions, arrangements or agreements with a director which, in the aggregate, did not exceed £5,000 and which are credit transactions or related to credit transactions.

1980 s 58(3)
(per 1981 3 sch 53)

(d) Transactions, arrangements or agreements (of the type envisaged by sections 54(1)(c) and 54(2)(c) of the Companies Act 1980) where the interest of a director did not exceed £1,000 during the year or, if more than £1,000, did not exceed the lower of £5,000 or 1 per cent of the net assets of the company at the end of the year.

1980 s 54(6)(d)

(e) Transactions or arrangements, or agreements relating thereto, which were made before 22 December 1980 and did not subsist on or after that day.

1980 s 54(7)   5.75

2. The requirements to disclose apply to all transactions or arrangements whether or not:

(a) they were unlawful;

(b) the person for whom they were made was either a director or connected person at the time of the transaction;

(c) a company was a subsidiary of a company other than its current holding company when they were made.

1981 1 sch 63(c), 68   5.86

3. Group accounts to show above information relating only to holding company directors.

Transactions with officers other than directors
1980 s 56(1)–(2)   5.87, 89

In respect of each of the following types of transactions (which should include related guarantees, securities, arrangements and agreements to enter into such transactions):

(a) loans;
(b) quasi-loans; and
(c) credit transactions;

1980 s 56(2)	made between the company (and, in the case of a holding company, its subsidiaries) and persons who were officers of the company at any time during the year, state for each type:

    (i)   the aggregate amount outstanding at the end of the year;

    (ii) the numbers of officers for whom such transactions or agreements were made.

1981 1 sch 58(3), 63(c)	Corresponding amounts need not be shown. Consolidated accounts need only include the information relating to holding company officers.

Note:

1980 s 56(2A) (per 1981 3 sch 52) 1980 s 56(3)	This does not apply to arrangements by recognised banks for their officers or their holding companies' officers. In addition, no disclosure necessary in respect of any officer if total due to company or group from him at year end re all such transactions less than £2,500.

Duty of auditors concerning loans to and other transactions with directors and officers

1980 s 59	5.74	Auditors to report, so far as they are reasonably able to do so, particulars which companies omit from their accounts in breach of the disclosure requirements above for transactions with directors and other officers.

Called up share capital not paid

1981 1 sch format note 1	5.91	Called up share capital not paid may be shown in either of the two positions in the standard formats.

Capital and Reserves

Called up share capital

1981 1 sch format note 12	5.93	Allotted share capital and paid up share capital to be shown separately.
1981 1 sch 38(1)	5.94	State authorised share capital, and number and total nominal value of shares of each class allotted.
1981 1 sch 40	5.95	In respect of any options on the unissued share capital state:

    (a) number, description and amount of shares involved;

    (b) period during which option is exercisable;

    (c) price to be paid for shares allotted.

| 1981 1 sch 60 | 5.96 | Number, description and amount of shares of the company held beneficially by subsidiaries to be shown by note. |

SSAP 8:28   5.97   State new fixed rate of dividend on preference shares issued before 6 April 1973.

1981 1 sch 38(2)   5.98   In the case of redeemable shares, show:

(a) earliest and latest dates of redemption;
(b) whether redemption is mandatory, or at the company's option;
(c) the amount of any premiums payable upon redemption.

Arrears of dividend
1981 1 sch 49   5.99   The amount and period of any arrears of fixed cumulative dividends are to be stated in the notes, exclusive of ACT, for each class of share.

Allotment of shares
1981 1 sch 39   5.100   If shares have been allotted in the year, state the reason and, for each class of share issued:

(a) description;
(b) number allotted;
(c) nominal value;
(d) aggregate consideration.

Reserves

Author   5.101   Reserves not to include any amounts properly considered to be provisions.

Author   5.102–103   Distinguish in the accounts between distributable and non-distributable reserves. Distributable reserves not set aside for any specific purpose should be combined with the profit and loss account.

Author   5.104   Non-distributable reserves not specifically identified in formats might be included as item AIV4.

1981 1 sch 46   5.105   A reconciliation is to be provided for all movements on reserves, showing:

(a) balance brought forward;
(b) transfers to and from the reserve;

(c) source and application respectively of those transfers; and

(d) the balance carried forward.

1981 1 sch 58(3)   A corresponding reconciliation for the previous year is not required.

SSAP 6:16   5.106   Transfers to or from retained profits and the application of other amounts to relieve charges on revenue are to be passed through the profit and loss account, except in the case of a material prior year adjustment.

Author   5.107   Balance on profit and loss account to be shown in position required by formats, even if a debit.

SSAP 4:9   5.108   If government grants are not deducted from the cost of an asset, but treated instead as a deferred credit, that deferred credit should be separately disclosed if material, but not as part of shareholders' funds.

SSAP 19:15   5.109   The investment property revaluation reserve is to be prominently displayed in the balance sheet.

Provisions for Liabilities and Charges

1981 1 sch 88   5.110   Provision is defined as amount retained to provide for future liability or loss which is either:

(a) likely to be incurred; or

(b) certain to be incurred, but uncertain as to amount or timing.

1981 1 sch 46   5.111   A reconciliation is to be provided for movements on such provisions, giving the following information:

(a) balance brought forward;
(b) transfers to and from the provision;
(c) source and application respectively of such transfers;
(d) balance carried foward;

1981 1 sch 58(3)   *unless* the only transfer is an application of the provision for the purpose for which it was established. Comparative figures are not required for these reconciliations.

Taxation provisions

1981 1 sch 47	5.112	The amount of any provision for taxation other than deferred taxation is to be stated.
		Give the following information about deferred tax by note:
SSAP 15:37	5.115	(a) Indicate the nature and amount of the major elements of which the net balance is composed, and describe the method of calculation adopted.
SSAP 15:38	5.113	(b) Where deferred taxation arises relating to movements on reserves, transfers to and from deferred taxation to be shown separately as part of such movements.
SSAP 15:39	5.114	(c) Where a note to the accounts states the value of an asset which differs from its book value, note is to show, if material, tax implication of realisation of asset at stated value.
SSAP 15:30	5.115	(d) Where only part of the full potential deferred tax is provided, the amount not provided should be based on substantiated calculations and assumptions which are explained in the accounts.
SSAP 15:33	5.118	(e) The full potential amount of deferred taxation for all timing differences should be disclosed by way of note, distinguishing between the various principal categories of deferred taxation and showing for each category the amount that has been provided within the accounts.

Pension funds

1981 1 sch 50(4)	5.144	Give details of any provision in balance sheet for pension commitments, showing separately commitments to past directors. State also details of commitments for which no provision made.
Author	5.145	Minimum recommended disclosure:
		(a) Extent to which employees covered.
		(b) Whether or not fund contributory.
		(c) Amount of any estimated underfunding.
		(d) Way in which underfunding (if any) is to be made good.

Creditors

General

| 1981 1 sch format note 13 | 5.119 | Amounts falling due within one year, and after one year, are to be shown separately for each item listed in standard format 2 under 'creditors', and separate totals are to be disclosed. |

1981 1 sch 48(1)   5.120–122   For each item included in creditors, disclose the amounts included which:

(a) are payable otherwise than by instalments more than five years hence;

(b) are payable by instalments any of which are due more than five years hence, and the total of such instalments;

1981 1 sch 48(2)–(3)   and state the terms of repayment and rates of interest payable. If statement is of excessive length, give general indication of terms and rates of interest.

1981 1 sch 48(4)   5.123   For each item in 'creditors' for which security has been given:

(a) state the amounts secured; and
(b) give general indication of security.

LA para 10(f)   5.124   State in respect of bank loans and overdrafts, and other borrowings, the aggregate amounts repayable:

(a) on demand or within one year;
(b) between one and two years hence;
(c) between two and five years hence;
(d) in five years or more.

Author   5.125   If company has exceeded any borrowing limits set by Articles or debenture trust deeds, disclose facts, amounts involved and action to be taken.

Debentures

1981 1 sch 41(1)   5.128   If debentures have been issued during the year, state:

(a) the reason for the issue;
(b) classes of debentures issued;
(c) for each class, the amount issued and the consideration received.

1981 1 sch 60	5.129	State number, description and amount of any holding company debentures in which a subsidiary was beneficially interested.
1981 1 sch format note 7	5.130	Show separately amount of any convertible loans.
1981 1 sch 41(2)	5.131	Give details of redeemed debentures which company has power to reissue.

Dividends

1981 1 sch 51(3)	5.132	State amount of provision for aggregate recommended dividend.
SSAP 8:26	5.133	ACT on above dividend not to be included with dividend, but included as a current tax liability.

Corporation tax

1981 1 sch format note 9, 13	5.134	Liabilities for taxation to be shown at item C8 and amount of 'any other creditors' to be shown separately.
SSAP 8:14		Disclose separately, if applicable:

    (a) the liability for mainstream corporation tax, being that on the profit of the year; and

    (b) the mainstream corporation tax on the profits of the previous year payable within nine months of the present balance sheet date.

SSAP 8:26–27	5.136, 138	Include the ACT on proposed dividends (whether recoverable or irrecoverable) as a current taxation liability. If it is considered to be recoverable, ACT should be deducted from deferred tax.

Payments received on account

1981 1 sch format note 8	5.140	To the extent that such payments are not deducted from stocks, disclose separately.

Accruals and deferred income

1981 1 sch format note 10	5.141	Show accruals and deferred income at any/all of the alternative positions as context requires.

Net current assets/liabilities

1981 1 sch format note 11	5.143	When format 1 is adopted, wherever 'prepayments and accrued income' shown, take into account in calculating net current assets.

Guarantees, commitments and contingencies

1981 1 sch 50(1)	5.146	Give details of charges on assets to secure liabilities of other persons, stating amounts if practicable.
1981 1 sch 50(2) SSAP 18:16, 18–19	5.147	Disclose amount, legal nature and security given for contingent liabilities not provided and not considered remote. In addition, state: (a) any uncertainties; (b) prudent estimate of effect, or statement that estimation is not practicable.
SSAP 18:20	5.148	Estimate of effect of contingencies to be disclosed before tax, and explain tax implications of crystallisation.
SSAP 18:17	5.149	Contingent gain only to be disclosed if probable that will be realised. Disclose as 5.147 and 5.148, except for security.
1981 1 sch 50(3)	5.150	Capital expenditure authorised but not yet contracted, and also capital expenditure contracted for.
1981 1 sch 50(5)	5.151	Details of other relevant commitments, not provided.
1981 1 sch 50(6)	5.153	In respect of above guarantees, commitments and pension funds, show separately commitments undertaken on behalf of: (a) subsidiaries; and (b) holding company or fellow subsidiaries.

Post balance sheet events

Author	5.156	If disclosure of non-adjusting post balance sheet events has been made in directors' report details may be omitted from notes. Cross reference may be thought helpful.

Ultimate holding company

1967 s 5	5.157	State name and country of incorporation of ultimate holding company.

Date of approval of accounts

SSAP 17:26	5.158	Date on which the accounts were approved by the directors should be stated.

PROFIT AND LOSS ACCOUNT

1981 1 sch format note 14, 17	6.7, 42	If format 1 or 3 is adopted, items 'cost of sales', 'distribution costs' and 'administrative expenses' are to be shown after taking account of any necessary depreciation, or provisions for diminution in value of assets. State total of such provisions by note.
SSAP 6:17	6.4	Statement of retained profits to follow profit and loss account, showing any prior year adjustments.
1981 1 sch 3(6), 7(a)–(b) SSAP 8:24	6.6	Show as separate items: (a) Profit or loss on ordinary activities before tax. (b) Transfers to or from reserves. (c) Aggregate net dividends paid and proposed, excluding ACT.
1981 1 sch format 1981 1 sch 57(2) SSAP 6:13, 15, 17	6.8	In the case of extraordinary items disclose: (a) result after tax before extraordinary items; (b) nature, particulars and amount of extraordinary items (less attributable taxation); (c) result after extraordinary items.
1981 1 sch 57(3) SSAP 6:5,14	6.9	Exceptional items deriving from the ordinary activities of the business are to be included in arriving at profit before tax and extraordinary items. State nature and amount.
1981 1 sch 57(1)	6.12	State effect of material amounts included in the current year's profit and loss account, but relating to prior years.
1981 1 sch 4(2) SSAP 6:16	6.11	Prior year adjustments to be effected by restatement of prior years and, as a result, reserves brought forward will be adjusted. Disclose effect by showing separately amount of restatement.
SSAP 12:6	6.10	Show material profit or loss on disposal of fixed assets.

Information supplementing the profit and loss account
Turnover and profit

1981 1 sch 94 SSAP 5:8	6.14	Turnover to be stated after deducting:

(a) VAT;
(b) trade discounts;
(c) other taxes based upon turnover.

1981 1 sch 55(1)	6.15	For each substantially different class of business, show:

(a) attributable turnover; and
(b) result before tax.

1981 1 sch 55(2)	6.17	Turnover attributable to each substantially different geographical market to be disclosed.

LA para 10(c)	6.18	If overseas trading accounts for more than 10 per cent of turnover, give:

(a) geographical analysis (in currency or percentages) of contributions to turnover derived from operations outside the UK and Eire; and

(b) similar analysis of trading results if abnormal contribution from individual regions.

If analysis required, analyse by continent. If one continent accounts for more than 50 per cent of overseas operations, further analysis required.

1981 1 sch 55(5)	6.21	If above information on turnover and profit omitted on grounds seriously prejudicial to company, state that fact.

Author	6.22	If a group company, consider disclosing sales to other group companies.

Rental and other income

1981 1 sch 53(5)	6.23	Property rental income net of rates etc to be shown if such rent a substantial part of total revenue.

1981 1 sch format note 15	6.26	Other interest receivable and similar income to be shown analysed between income from group companies and other sources.

Author	6.27	If material government revenue-based grants have been credited to revenue, state fact and amount.

Investment income

1981 1 sch 53(4) SSAP 8:25	6.24	Show income from listed investments, including tax credit in the case of franked investment income.
1981 1 sch format note 15	6.25	Income from fixed asset investments to be shown analysed between income from group companies and other sources.

Income from related companies

SSAP 1:10, 14–17	6.44	Include in investing group's consolidated profit and loss account the group's aggregate share of profits less losses of related companies. Disclose separately group's aggregate share of related companies':

    (a)   profits less losses before tax;
    (b)   tax (within group tax charge);
    (c)   extraordinary items (to be aggregated with group extraordinary items unless material);
    (d)   net profits less losses retained.

SSAP 1:8 Author	6.47–49	If investing company does not prepare consolidated accounts, profit and loss account to be adapted to include share of related companies' profits less losses as above. Share of retained profits to be transferred to revaluation reserve. If investment not valued under equity method, disclose investor's share of retained revenues by note.
SSAP 1:18	6.44	If the results of one or more related companies are individually of such significance that more detailed information about these would assist in giving a true and fair view, show separately:

    (a)   total turnover;
    (b)   total depreciation charge;
    (c)   total profits less losses before taxation; and
    (d)   the amounts of such profits attributable to the investing company or group.

Author	6.50	'Income from shares in related companies' — i.e. dividend income — to be shown separately from share of related company profits. Such share of profits to be described by an alternative name on the face of the profit and loss account.

Auditors' remuneration

1981 1 sch 53(7)   6.28

Auditors' remuneration, including expenses, to be disclosed. In consolidated accounts, state consolidated remuneration.

Hire of plant and machinery

1981 1 sch 53(6)   6.52

Hire charges for plant and machinery to be stated.

Interest payable and similar charges

1981 1 sch format note 16   6.51
1981 1 sch 53(2)

Interest payable and similar charges to be split in accounts between payable to group companies and the rest. Show separately by note:

(a) interest on bank loans and overdrafts and other loans from non-group entities which are either:

  (i) not repayable by instalments, and are due within five years; or
  (ii) repayable by instalments wholly due within five years; and

(b) interest on any other loans from non-group entities.

Depreciation

1981 1 sch 19(1)–(3)   6.42

State:

(a) provision against fixed asset investments for diminutions in value;

(b) provisions against fixed assets for permanent diminutions in value;

(c) write-back of provisions made under (a) or (b) above, when no longer required.

Directors' emoluments

1948 s 196(1)–(5), (7)   6.29–30

State aggregate amounts paid by company (or group) for services as director and other services in each of the following categories:

(a) Directors' fees and emoluments.
(b) Pensions.
(c) Compensation for loss of office to past directors.

Amounts above to be those paid by the company (and its subsidiaries and other parties) and in the case of (c) analyse between paid by company, by subsidiaries, and by other parties.

| 1948 s 196(6) | 6.31 | Show separately within the above: |

(a) amounts of monies received not accounted for to company within two years; and

(b) expense allowances subsequently charged to tax.

| 1967 s 6(1)–(2), (6)
1967 s 7(1), (3)
SI 1979 No 1618
LA para 10(m) | 6.33–34 | If total directors' emoluments exceed £40,000 or if holding or subsidiary company, then show: |

(a) chairman's emoluments;

(b) emoluments of highest paid director, if in excess of chairman;

(c) number of directors whose emoluments fall into each £5,000 bracket;

(d) number of directors waiving emoluments, and total amount waived. Listed companies to give details of waivers of future emoluments (whether receivable from company or subsidiaries).

For the purposes of this paragraph, £40,000 relates to the amount required to be shown by virtue of 1948 s 196(1) (i.e. all fees, emoluments and compensations) but excludes pension contributions paid on a director's behalf.

| 1981 1 sch 63(a) | 6.35 | For consolidated accounts, details relating to directors of holding company only need be disclosed. |

| 1948 s 196(8)
1967 s 6(4), 7(3) | 6.38 | Auditors to disclose above directors' emoluments if accounts do not. |

Employees' emoluments

| 1967 s 8
SI 1979 No 1618
1981 1 sch 63(b) | 6.36–37 | Number of employees (excluding directors) whose emoluments exceed £20,000, in bands of £5,000. In group accounts, employees of holding company only. |

| 1967 s 8(4) | 6.38 | Auditors to disclose above employees' emoluments if accounts do not. |

Staff

1981 1 sch 56(1), (5)	6.39–40	State:

    (a)   average number of employees (wherever employed) in the year; and

    (b)   average number of employees analysed into categories appropriate to the business.

.Author .   Indicate whether or not executive directors included in above.

1981 1 sch 56(4)   6.41   In respect of the above employees, if not disclosed in profit and loss account, state:

    (a)   aggregate wages and salaries;

    (b)   social security costs incurred by the company on their behalf; and

    (c)   other pension costs incurred.

Author   Indicate whether or not executive directors included in above.

Taxation

1981 1 sch 54   6.54–55   Charge for year to be shown distinguishing:
SSAP 8:22
SSAP 15:34, 36

    (a)   UK corporation tax, stating basis, showing double tax relief separately;

    (b)   transfers to/from deferred tax;

    (c)   UK income tax (i.e. tax attributable to franked investment income);

    (d)   overseas taxation (relieved and unrelieved) on profits, income and (if applicable) capital gains. Show that part of unrelieved overseas taxation attributable to dividend payment;

    (e)   'irrecoverable' ACT.

1981 1 sch 54(3)   6.54   Items (a), (c) and (d) above to be split between tax on ordinary
SSAP 15:36   activities and on extraordinary items.

SSAP 8:23	6.56	Disclose rate of corporation tax used.
SSAP 6:5	6.57	Adjustments in respect of prior year tax charge to be included (normally) in charge for year, but disclosed separately if material.
Author	6.58	If material trading losses set off against chargeable gains, show true incidence of tax suffered and relieved.
1981 1 sch 54(2)	6.59	Disclose special circumstances affecting tax liability in current or future years.
SSAP 15:35	6.60	State extent to which tax charge reduced by accelerated capital allowances, other timing differences and stock relief.
SSAP 15:36	6.61	Disclose adjustments to deferred tax due to change in rate of tax as part of charge for year. If associated with fundamental change in tax system, then show as extraordinary item.

Dividends

1981 1 sch 3(7)(b) SSAP 8:24	6.62	Show aggregate dividends paid and proposed, excluding ACT and tax credit.
1981 1 sch 51(3) Author	6.63	Distinguish dividends by class of shares and whether paid or proposed. State dividend rate per cent, or pence per share.

Redemption of loans and share capital

1981 1 sch 53(3)	6.64	State amounts set aside for redemption of share capital and loans respectively.

Earnings per share — listed companies only

SSAP 3:14	6.65	Earnings per share ('eps') on 'net' basis, with comparative for previous period, to be shown on face of profit and loss account.
SSAP 3:9	6.66	If materially different from above, show also eps on 'nil distribution' basis.
SSAP 3:15	6.67	Show basis of calculation of eps and particularly amount of earnings, and number of shares used.
SSAP 3:16	6.68	Fully diluted eps to be disclosed as well as basic eps if more than 5 per cent different from basic eps and: (a) there is share capital which does not currently rank for dividend, but will do so in the future; or

(b) the company has issued debentures, loan stock or preference shares convertible into equity shares; or

(c) options or warrants granting the right to subscribe for the company's equity capital have been issued.

SSAP 3:16   6.69   If fully diluted eps is disclosed, show:

(a) the basis of calculation; and
(b) comparative figures, if applicable.

Give fully diluted eps equal prominence with the basic eps.

STATEMENT OF SOURCE AND APPLICATION OF FUNDS

General

SSAP 10:9   7.1   SSAP 10 applies to accounts intended to give a true and fair view, other than those of enterprises with turnover or gross income of less than £25,000 per annum.

SSAP 10:10–11   7.1, 3   Accounts should, subject to the above, include a statement of source and application of funds both for the period under review and for the corresponding previous period. The statement should show the profit or loss for the period together with the adjustments required for items which did not use (or provide) funds in the period.

SSAP 10:11   7.4   The following other sources and applications of funds should, where material, also be shown:

(a) Dividends paid.

(b) Acquisitions and disposals of fixed and other non-current assets.

(c) Funds raised by increasing, or expended in repaying or redeeming, medium or long term loans or the issued capital of the company.

(d) Increase or decrease in working capital, subdivided into its components, and movements in net liquid funds.

SSAP 16:62   7.2   Where the main accounts are current cost accounts, the statement should be compatible with those accounts.

Group accounts

SSAP 10:12	7.5	Where the accounts are those of a group, the statement of source and application of funds should be so framed as to reflect the operations of the group. Where a consolidated statement is provided, a statement in respect of the holding company is not required.
SSAP 10:5	7.6	Show effects of acquisition or disposal of subsidiaries, and how funded, differentiating between consideration satisfied in cash and by issue of shares.

GROUP ACCOUNTS

Legal requirement for group accounts

1948 s 150(1), (2)(a) SSAP 14:15, 19	8.1, 9	Group accounts to be submitted if company had subsidiaries at year end, and not itself wholly owned subsidiary of company incorporated in Great Britain. Explain basis on which subsidiaries included.
1948 s 151(1)–(2) 1981 1 sch 61 SSAP 14:2, 10, 15, 22	8.4–6	Group accounts will normally consist of a single set of consolidated financial statements. However, equivalent information may be given in some other way if directors consider it more informative. Directors should justify their use of any alternative to consolidated accounts.
1981 1 sch 68	8.7	Group accounts not prepared as consolidated accounts to give same or equivalent information as if they had been consolidated accounts.
1948 s 150(2)(b)	8.10–11	A subsidiary may be omitted from group accounts if directors consider inclusion would:

(a) be impracticable;
(b) be of no real value, due to immateriality of sums involved;
(c) involve expense or delay out of proportion to value;
(d) be misleading;
(e) be harmful to the business of company or subsidiaries (DoT approval needed);
(f) be meaningless on grounds of different business. (DoT approval needed.)

If all subsidiaries omitted on these grounds, group accounts not required.

SSAP 14:20	8.12–14	Consider whether group accounts omitting subsidiaries give a true and fair view. If group accounts not produced, or subsidiaries excluded, state:
1981 1 sch 69(2)(a)		(a) reasons for exclusion;
1981 1 sch 69(2)(b)		(b) material audit qualifications or other items to which attention is drawn in the accounts of subsidiaries, unless dealt with in holding company's own accounts;
1981 1 sch 69(3)–(4)		(c) aggregate amount of holding company's or group's investment in subsidiaries, on equity basis. May be excluded if directors state in the notes that value of these investments is not less than value shown in accounts — the investor company being the wholly owned subsidiary or another Great Britain company;
1981 1 sch 69(5)		(d) if above information not obtainable, state so.
1948 s 149(5)–(6) (per 1981 s 1(1))	8.15	Holding company need not publish separate profit and loss account if the consolidated accounts show how much of consolidated result is attributable to holding company, and contain a note that no separate profit and loss account is submitted.

Consolidated accounts

1981 1 sch 61	8.18	Consolidated accounts to combine separate accounts, but with such adjustments as directors see fit.
1981 1 sch 62–63	8.18–19	Consolidated accounts to comply with requirements as if the accounts of a single company, except that the following information need be given in respect of the holding company only:
1948 s 196, 1967 s 6–7		(a) Directors' emoluments, pensions and compensation payments.
1980 s 54, 56		(b) Transactions with directors and other officers.
1967 s 4		(c) Certain investments in other companies.
1967 s 8		(d) Employees' emoluments in excess of £20,000.
1981 s 4		(e) Financial information about subsidiaries and related companies.

| SSAP 14:21 | 8.22 | A subsidiary is to be excluded from consolidation if: |

(a) its activities so dissimilar from 'rest of group as to be misleading;

(b) holding company controls more than half the equity capital but:

    (i) does not have control of half the voting capital; or
    (ii) cannot for contractual or other reasons control the board;

(c) subsidiary operates under severe restrictions that impair control; or

(d) control is intended to be temporary.

| SSAP 14:23 | 8.23 | In the case of exclusion due to dissimilar activities, include in group accounts separate financial statements for subsidiary and state: |

(a) holding company's interest;

(b) intra group balances;

(c) nature of transactions with rest of group;

(d) reconciliation with group's investment in subsidiary as shown in consolidated accounts, which should be stated on equity basis.

| SSAP 14:24 | 8.24 | If excluded from consolidation on grounds of lack of effective control, account for subsidiary as either: |

(a) a related company if SSAP 1 satisfied; or
(b) an investment.

| SSAP 14:25–26 | 8.25 | If subsidiary operates under severe restrictions, include in consolidated balance sheet at equity valuation at date restrictions came into force, less any provision for permanent diminution in value, and disclose: |

(a) net assets;
(b) results for year;
(c) amounts included in consolidated profit and loss for dividends received, and to write down investment.

SSAP 14:27	8.26	If control is temporary, show as current asset at lower of cost and net realisable value.
SSAP 14:28	8.27	In all cases where subsidiary excluded from consolidated accounts state: (a) reasons; (b) names of principal subsidiaries involved; (c) premium or discount on acquisition not written off; (d) any other information required by the Companies Acts.
SSAP 14:22	8.6	If SSAP 14 provides for subsidiary to be excluded from consolidated accounts, but it is included, directors to justify and state reasons.
SSAP 1:17 Author	8.20	Statement analysing the retained profit for the year between amounts attributable to the holding company, subsidiaries and related companies, should immediately follow the profit and loss account.
SSAP 14:34	8.28	Minority interests to be shown separately from shareholders' funds. Only include a debit balance if binding obligation upon minority to contribute.
SSAP 14:36	8.21	State effect of restrictions on distribution of retained profits.
SSAP 14:35	8.29	Show minority interest in group profit or loss after tax but before extraordinary items on the face of the profit and loss account.
SSAP 14:16	8.31	If it is impractical to adopt group accounting policies in respect of a subsidiary, or to adjust on consolidation, disclose: (a) different policies used; (b) amounts of assets and liabilities involved; (c) an indication, if practicable, of the likely effect; (d) the reasons for the different treatment.
SSAP 14:18 1981 1 sch 70	8.33, 35	If subsidiaries' accounts (whether or not included in group accounts) not coterminous with or same length as those of holding company notes to the accounts to state: (a) names of principal subsidiaries concerned; (b) reasons; (c) dates of last year end before that of holding company;

(d) accounting period involved if not same length as holding company's.

If information at (c) of excessive length, give earliest and latest such dates.

SSAP 14:30   8.36   If material changes in group, show enough information to enable shareholders to understand effect on consolidated results.

CURRENT COST ACCOUNTS AND THE ALTERNATIVE ACCOUNTING RULES

1981 1 sch 29–34   9.5   If main accounts are prepared on anything other than pure historical cost basis, alternative accounting rules must be followed.

Author   9.3   Main accounts may take one of three forms:

(a) pure historical cost accounts ('HC'); or
(b) historical cost accounts with asset revaluations; or
(c) current cost ('CC') accounts.

SSAP 16:48   9.4   Companies to which SSAP 16 applies should attach appropriate supplementary accounts.

Provisions common to SSAP 16 and the alternative accounting rules

1981 1 sch 33(2)   9.8   State valuation bases and methods adopted in respect of:
SSAP 16:58

(a) fixed assets and depreciation;
(b) stocks and work in progress;
(c) current asset investments.

Provisions contained only in alternative accounting rules

1981 1 sch 33(3)–(4)   9.12   If assets (other than stocks) are included at other than historical cost, state:

(a) historical cost amount; or
(b) difference between historical cost amount and balance sheet amount;

1981 1 sch 43   and except in the case of listed investments:

(c) years in which assets valued and various values; and
(d) for assets valued in year, names or qualifications of valuers, and bases of valuation used.

1981 1 sch 32(3)	9.13	If main accounts are CC accounts, HC depreciation charge may be shown on face of profit and loss account, and depreciation adjustment by way of note.
1981 1 sch 34(4)	9.14	Revaluation reserve is to be reduced if directors no longer consider it necessary for purpose of company's accounting policies. Transfer may only be made to profit and loss account if:

(a) amount was previously charged to that account; or
(b) amount represents realised profit.

1981 1 sch 34(5)	9.15	State tax treatment of items charged or credited to revaluation reserve.

Provisions contained only in SSAP 16

SSAP 16:46	9.16–17	CC accounts are to be included in all financial statements intended to show a true and fair view, unless the entity falls into one of the categories below:

(a) no class of share or loan capital is listed on a stock exchange, and two of the following three criteria are met:

  (i) turnover less than £5,000,000;
  (ii) balance sheet totals at commencement of year per HC accounts less than £2,500,000;
  (iii) average number of UK employees less than 250; or

(b) wholly owned subsidiary of UK or Eire registered company; or

(c) (i) authorised insurers; or
  (ii) property investment or dealing entity;
  (iii) unit or investment trust companies etc; or

(d) primary financial aim is not to make an operating profit.

However, if holding company is itself exempt by (c) or (d) above, but has non-exempt subsidiaries and non-exempt part of group exceeds criteria at (a) above, CC accounts are required for non-exempt part of group.

SSAP 16:47, 60–61	9.18	Supplementary CC accounts should contain a profit and loss account, balance sheet, explanatory notes and comparative figures. If consolidated CC statements produced, and holding

company's main accounts are HC accounts, company need not produce its own CC accounts.

SSAP 16:55	9.19	The CC profit and loss account should contain the following information, as a minimum:

(a) CC operating profit.
(b) Interest/income from net borrowing.
(c) Gearing adjustment.
(d) Taxation.
(e) Extraordinary items.
(f) CC result after tax and extraordinary items, attributable to shareholders.

SSAP 16:56	9.20	Unless shown on the face of the profit and loss account, provide reconciliation between CC and HC operating profits, stating:

(a) depreciation adjustment;
(b) cost of sales adjustment;
(c) monetary working capital adjustment;
(d) other material adjustments.

Adjustments (b) and (c) above may be combined.

SSAP 16:59	9.21	Listed companies to state CC earnings per share.
SSAP 16:57	9.24	Notes to the balance sheet should disclose:

(a) total net operating assets;
(b) net borrowing;
(c) main elements in (a) and (b) above;
(d) movements in fixed assets;
(e) movements on reserves.

SSAP 16:58	9.25	Notes to describe methods adopted in relation to:

(a) cost of sales adjustment;
(b) monetary working capital adjustment;
(c) foreign currency translation;
(d) gearing adjustment;
(e) other material adjustments;
(f) comparative figures.

Investment Properties

SSAP 19 part 4 1948 s 149(4) (per 1981 s 1(1))	9.27	If investment properties carried at market value and not depreciated, give particulars of departure from alternative accounting rules, reasons for it, and effect.

MISCELLANEOUS DISCLOSURES

1948 s 155(1)	11.24	Balance sheet to be signed by two directors, or if only one director, by that person.
Stock Exchange	11.32	Listed companies recommended to disclose:

    (a)   table of comparative figures for last 5 or 10 years; and
    (b)   principal products.

Abridged accounts

1981 s 11(6)–(9)	10.5	If abridged accounts are published, state:

    (a)   that accounts are not full accounts;
    (b)   whether full accounts have been filed with registrar;
    (c)   whether audit opinion expressed on full accounts;
    (d)   whether or not such opinion was unqualified.

The auditors' report on full accounts is not to be attached.

MODIFIED ACCOUNTS

Eligibility

1981 s 5(3)–(5)	10.12–13	Exemptions from filing accounts are available to 'small' or 'medium sized' companies or groups unless:

    (a)   for companies, any of the following apply:

        (i)   public company;
        (ii)   banking, insurance or shipping company;
        (iii)   member of ineligible group;

    (b)   for groups, any member is:

        (i)   public company;
        (ii)   banking, insurance or shipping company (including recognised or licensed banking institutions);
        (iii)   body corporate (other than a company) with power to offer shares or debentures to the public.

Size criteria for modified accounts

| 1981 s 8(1)–(3) | 10.6 | To be classified as small or medium sized, company or group to satisfy at least two of following: |

		Small	*Medium*
(a)	Annual turnover not exceeding	£1,400,000	£5,750,000
(b)	Balance sheet total not exceeding	£700,000	£2,800,000
(c)	Average number of employees not exceeding	50	250

| 1981 s 8(5)–(6) | 10.8–9 | If small or medium sized in one year, entitled regardless of size in following year to present modified accounts to registrar. Exemption does not apply to year after such a year, unless size restrictions are again met. |

Small company exemptions

| 1981 s 6(2) | 10.14 | Following are not required to be filed: |

(a) Profit and loss account.
(b) Directors' report.

| 1981 s 6(2)–(5) | 10.14–16 | Modified balance sheet and notes may be submitted, as follows: |

(a) Balance sheet — show only headings prefixed with Roman numerals, except that debtors and creditors are to be analysed between amounts due and not due within one year.

(b) Notes need only include the information in 1981 1 sch, as it relates to:

(i) accounting policies;
(ii) share capital;
(iii) particulars of allotments;
(iv) particulars of debts;
(v) foreign currency translation;
(vi) comparative figures.

| 1948 s 196 | | Details of directors' and employees' emoluments are not required. |
| 1967 s 6–8 | | |

Note:
Other statutory disclosures (e.g. relating to loans to directors) found outside 1981 1 sch must still be made.

Medium sized company exemptions

1981 s 6(7)(a)–(b), (8)	10.17–18	Modified profit and loss account permitted. Balance sheet etc required in full. Profit and loss account (or related notes):

(a) need not show details of turnover;

(b) may combine into one item called 'gross profit or loss':

    (i)   in format 1, items 1, 2, 3 and 6;
    (ii)   in format 2, items 1 to 5;
    (iii) in format 3, items A1, B1 and B2; and
    (iv) in format 4, items A1, A2 and B1 to B4.

Small and medium sized companies — general

1981 s 7(1)	10.19	Modified accounts to be signed by at least two directors, or if only one director, by that person.

1981 s 7(2)–(3)	10.20	Statement to be made above directors' signatures that they:

(a) have relied upon the exemptions for individual accounts;
(b) have done so on grounds that company is entitled to benefit from exemptions as a small or medium sized company (state which).

1981 s 7(4), (5)(a)–(b)	10.21	Modified accounts to include a special auditors' report:

(a) stating that exemption requirements have been met; and
(b) reproducing full text of auditors' report on the full accounts.

Group accounts exemption

1981 s 9–10	10.22–26	Modified accounts may be filed for both holding company and the group provided that the holding company is itself entitled to and has taken advantage of the exemptions. In considering the size criteria, use consolidated accounts, adjusted for unconsolidated subsidiaries. Holding company may only file modified accounts if group would also qualify. If group medium sized, holding company may only benefit from medium sized company exemptions, even if it would otherwise be considered 'small'.

1981 s 10(5)	10.27	The directors' statement made on the holding company balance sheet must include statement that modified group accounts also filed.

Dormant companies

| 1981 s 12(10)–(11) | 10.30 | Directors to state that company was dormant throughout the year on face of any unaudited balance sheet. |

Index

Index

Index